Spine-Chilling Murders in San Francisco

Copyright © 2022 / 2023 Nick Vulich

Nick Vulich

Table of Contents

The Demon of the Belfry (1895)

Catherine Stevens, Lila Berry, and Mrs. Nolte discovered Minnie Williams's body in the library of the Emanuel Baptist Church on April 14, 1898. The women had planned to decorate the church for the Easter celebration. However, when they arrived, Mrs. Nolte wanted to see the library, so they went in.

They found a woman's battered, partially naked body in a small room off the church library. It lay on its back, covered in blood, with the clothing in disarray.

The girl's right hand was nearly severed. In addition, she had a huge gash across her forehead and two more wounds on her chest where her clothes were cut off. When the medical examiner checked the girl's mouth, he discovered her underwear had been stuffed down her throat, gagging her.

And then, after she was dead, the killer stabbed her in the chest repeatedly with a silver table knife. The broken blade lay near the body.

There was no evidence of a struggle, so detectives assumed the attack likely came as a complete surprise.

The victim was quickly identified as Minnie Williams, age 21, a small, frail girl weighing only ninety pounds. She was a member of the Alameda Baptist Church and was just in town for the day to attend the Easter service at the Emanuel Baptist Church.

Charles Hills recalled seeing William Durrant and Minnie Williams standing on the corner of Bartlett and Twenty-third Streets. He heard Durrant say, "Oh, come along. What are you afraid of?" They walked to the church. The man opened the basement door, and they went inside.

Later that night, Durrant was at the church social at about 10:30 p.m. No one recalled seeing Minnie Williams.

After Minnie Williams' body was found, detectives wondered if there might be a connection with Blanche Lamont. She had disappeared a few weeks before. The girls were members of the same Sunday school class and ran in the same circle of friends.

Minnie Williams's partially naked body was found in the library of the Emanuel Church. She was a small, frail girl who weighed less than ninety pounds. (San Francisco Call. April 14, 1895.)

Durrant matched the description of the man seen with Blanche at the Powell Street car. He was 25 and had black hair and a black mustache.

Blanche was 21, with brown hair, large brown eyes, and a big girlish smile. The papers said she was "very pretty." She lived with her aunt, Mrs. Charles G. Noble, while studying to be a teacher at the Normal School.

6

The following day, Detective Ed Gibson and Officer Riehl found Blanche Lamont's body in the church belfry, just above the room where Minnie Williams's body was discovered. They had searched the church the previous night but could not get in the belfry, so they returned in the morning.

"The body was stark naked," said Detective Ed Gibson. "There was not a stitch of clothing on it or nearby. The body was laid on its back as if for burial, and no undertaker could have done it better. A tiny pool of blood stained the floor below her mouth."[1]

The body was beginning to turn black and decompose, so he guessed it had been there for about ten days. Maybe longer.

Halfway up the stairs to the belfry, detectives found a large pool of blood that had soaked through the treads and risers. That indicated the killer had stopped for a short rest before lugging the body up the stairs.

Detectives figured Blanche Lamont was murdered in the same room as Minnie Williams. After strangling the girl, the killer dragged the body up the stairs to the belfry.

The stairs were narrow, and there was little to no light, so the killer must have backed up the stairs, dragging the body, groping the wall for support

After killing the girl, he shredded her clothes. Then he climbed twenty feet up into the steeple and hid her garments in the beams.

Blanche Lamont disappeared on April 3, 1895. She was last seen with W. H. Theodore Durrant, a dental student at Cooper Medical College. (San Francisco Call. April 15, 1895.)

Even then, the killer wasn't satisfied he'd hidden his trail. So, he removed the doorknobs and sealed the belfry door shut, hoping to keep intruders out.

Friends described Blanche as a "wholesome, healthy girl of a strong, well-filled frame." She had "romantic ideas" and a "foolish girl's longing for strange adventures."[2] In this case, those traits likely led her to her death. The papers said Blanche was uncommonly strong for a woman and would have put up a hell of a fight. She stood five feet eight and weighed 150 pounds.

Blanche dropped out of sight on April 3 and was not seen again until her body was found on April 14.

Suspicion quickly fell on W. H. Theodore Durrant, a dental student at Cooper Medical College in San Francisco.

The thing was, Durrant wasn't someone you'd suspect of being a killer. He was active in the Emanuel Baptist Church and served as the church librarian and secretary for the Christian Endeavor Youth group. Durrant was also a member of the National Guard, serving as a trumpeter in the Second Brigade Signal Corps.

And yet, all signs pointed to Theodore Durrant as the killer.

The police arrested Durrant at the foot of Mount Diablo on April 14. The case against him was circumstantial, but the pieces were coming together.

Durrant didn't have much to say to the press when he was brought in. "Yes, I know there are some circumstances against me," he said, "but they will be explained to Chief Crowley."[3]

Later, when he got to the jail, Durrant opened up to friends and reporters.

He left home at about 8 a.m. the day Blanche Lamont disappeared. He was going to George King's place to help with some wiring.

He met Blanche on the way and hopped onto a streetcar with her. They talked about a new book he was reading, *William Makepeace Thackeray's, The Newcombe's*. Durrant promised to bring it to her. That was the last he saw of her.

He hadn't seen Minnie Williams in at least three weeks.

That may be. But unfortunately, Durrant had a key to the church. He was seen letting Minnie Williams in the church's basement door the day before her body was found in the church library. Then later that evening, he arrived late for the church reception. His clothes were disheveled, and someone recalled seeing blood on them. Finally, perhaps most damning, Minnie Williams's purse was found in his overcoat when the detective's searched his parent's home.

Minnie William's purse was the primary evidence the police had against Durrant. Durrant told Chief Crowley he found it on the sidewalk but wasn't sure who it belonged to. Then he told Detective Seymour that he found it at Bartlett and Twenty-second Streets and then at Twenty-third and Twenty-fourth streets.

Henry Durrant wasn't someone you'd suspect of being a killer. He was active in the Emanuel Baptist Church and served as the church librarian and secretary for the Christian Endeavor Youth group. (San Francisco Call. December 7, 1895.)

The only answer for the discrepancy was that he was confused or lying. Police suspected the latter.

Coroner's inquest

At the coroner's inquest, it came out that Theodore Durrant and several other young men had been using the Emanuel Baptist Church as their playhouse. The side entrance to the church acted as a revolving door, letting women into the church at all hours. From all indications, Durrant was an oversexed pervert, inviting women to play doctor or——

The two victims weren't the first parishioners Theodore Durrant had tried to lure into the building. Lucille Turner, "a tall, handsome woman," testified that she had known Durrant for a year and was a member of the Christian Endeavor Society.

Durrant tried to entice her into the church the previous month. She had been feeling sickly, and he offered to play doctor and examine her. Durrant said he knew a place in the church where no one would disturb them. Lucille turned him down and walked away.

Later, at the trial, Budd Wilson, a neighborhood handyman, said Theodore Durrant and George King took girls to the church every night. He knew of at least five girls who went there with them.

"They all belong to respectable families," said Wilson. "Their parents never dreamed that such things were going on."[4]

Next up was Dr. Julius Rosenstirn. He gave a brief and titillating overview of sadism, telling the jury that it was a disease. A "form of sexual insanity that does not affect the reasoning power. After the commission of a crime, a sadist possesses all the cunning of a perfectly sane man in hiding the traces of his crime."

"The victim is never mutilated first," continued Rosenstirn. "This is because the frenzy of the sadist has not been satisfied."

Whatever the case warned Rosenstirn, sadism "should not be received as an excuse for murder. Punishment should be promptly meted out to all such persons."[5]

Several people testified they saw Blanche Lamont talking to a man the night she disappeared. It might have been Theodore Durrant, but they couldn't say for sure.

Cecilia and Maggie Fitzpatrick walked along Twenty-second Street with Emma and Louisa Struven. Suddenly, a man walked over to them. He called out, "Flora," looked into their eyes, then walked away.

The man wore a long overcoat and had a soft hat pulled down over his eyes. And even though it was dark, and his eyes were covered, the girls were sure it was Durrant.

At the coroner's inquest, it came out that Theodore Durrant had been using the Emanuel Baptist Church as his playhouse. The side entrance to the church acted as a revolving door, letting women into the church at all hours. (San Francisco Call. November 6, 1895.)

Tryphena Noble, Blanche Lamont's aunt, testified that Blanche was "very friendly" with Durrant. "They met frequently," said Noble, "and Durrant was very attentive to my niece."[6]

Durrant proposed to Blanche a few weeks before Christmas, but she didn't think he meant it. She just laughed. He kept asking her, and finally, she stopped going out with him. Rumor had it he was engaged to another woman.

Adolph Oppenheim, a pawn shop operator on DuPont Street, testified that sometime between April 4 and 10, Durrant tried to sell him one of Blanche's rings. However, he didn't buy it because it was too small.[7]

And then, several clues seemed to prove Durrant wasn't the killer. A woman testified she heard screams from inside the church at 10 p.m. on the night Minnie Williams died. But that wasn't possible. Several witnesses placed Durrant at Dr. Vogel's house at that time.

The police found footprints in the dust in the church belfry. They showed that the man wore a size 8 or 9 shoe, and Durrant wore a size 6. So, if those clues were accurate, Theodore Durrant was innocent.[8]

Finally, Chief Crowley discounted the footprint evidence, saying the police had never taken footprints. It's possible, but it's just as likely he was tightening up his case, eliminating loose ends.[9]

And then, there was talk that Durrant performed an abortion on Blanche Lamont and bungled it. Rather than explain what happened, he killed her.

Dr. Barrett, the autopsy physician, quickly put that theory to rest. He had spent five hours examining Blanche's body. She was not pregnant, and no operation had been performed on her, criminal or otherwise.[10] However, Barrett confirmed that both women were outraged just before they were killed.[11] Newspapers couldn't say sexually assaulted or raped at the turn of the century. It was always "criminally assaulted" or "outraged."

That was the case against Durrant for Blanche Lamont's murder. Next, the coroner took up Minnie Williams's case.

Minnie William's father said she was on friendly terms with Theodore Durrant. She was going with him, but Durrant was going with several other girls. Moreover, she told him, Durrant was "not altogether straight." And then, a girl told her something that further aroused her suspicions.[12] So, she decided that dating Theodore Durrant was a dead end.

Finally, Williams identified the pocket book found in Durrant's coat as one he'd given his daughter.

Dr. F. H. Shank examined Minnie Williams's body. She was dead before the killer mutilated her body. "Moreover, the splashes on the wall were thrown there and not ejected from the wounds in the body."

He couldn't imagine why the killer did it unless he wanted to throw the blame on a robber or a lunatic.

Or maybe, Durrant left the girl for dead and went to Dr. Vogel's party. Then, after midnight, when the party ended, Durrant returned to the church and found the girl alive. So, he finished the job. That would explain why there was no blood on Durrant when he arrived at the party.

Of course, it was only a theory. Dr. Shank couldn't say what happened until they found the killer's clothes.[13] Then, the blood stains would tell the story.

At the end of the hearing, Judge Carroll Conlan ordered Durrant to be held without bail.

Trial

Theodore Durrant was tried before Judge Murphy beginning on September 3, 1895. The prosecution decided to try him for the murder of Blanche Lamont because the evidence was stronger.

District Attorney William Barnes painted a picture of Durrant as an animal stalking his prey as he detailed Blanche's final moments.

The bodies of two female parishioners were found in the Emanuel Baptist Church on Bartlett Street in San Francisco. Both women were criminally assaulted, then strangled to death. (San Francisco Call. April 14, 1895.)

Blanche and Durrant rode the cars to the boy's high school on Sutter Street, where she got off. Durrant continued on his way to Cooper Medical College. And then, when Blanche finished her studies at the high school, she went to the Normal School to attend a cooking class.

Durrant paced outside the school for nearly an hour, waiting for her to leave.

Blanche and fellow student, Minnie Belle Edwards, walked together toward the Powell Street car. Durrant walked up to Blanche, raised his hat, and spoke for a few moments. Then they got in the car and sat together.

Two other students, Alice Pleasant and May Lannigan saw them sitting in the car as they walked by.

Attorney Martin Quinlan watched the couple transfer to the Valencia Street car. And then, at 4 p.m., he saw them walking on Twenty-first Street in the direction of the Emanuel Baptist Church. Another witness, Caroline Leak, watched them stroll by from her window.

They arrived at the gate leading to the side door of the church at 4:20 p.m. Durrant opened the gate, followed Blanche through it, and then closed it.

George R. King, the church organist, arrived at 5 p.m., entering through the main door on Bartlett Street. He noticed a gassy smell and walked around searching for the source. He checked the library and then locked the door behind him.

After King was satisfied there was no leak, he sat down at the piano. A few minutes later, Theodore Durrant stumbled in without his hat or coat, looking pale and disheveled.

Theodore Durrant in the county jail shortly after his arrest on April 15, 1895. (San Francisco Call. April 15, 1895.)

Durrant looked "ghastly," exclaimed King. "His hair was disheveled, his eyes bloodshot, and his face pale."[14]

Durrant said he'd been on top of the church fixing the electrical wires when he'd been overcome by escaping gas. He gave King a half dollar and asked him to get some Bromo-seltzer at the drugstore.

When King returned, Durrant took the Bromo-seltzer. Then they carried a small organ into the Sunday school. When they entered the library, they found Durrant's coat and hat. (The prosecutor stopped for a moment, emphasizing that the garments weren't there when King first entered the library. However, the hat and coat mysteriously appeared after King returned from the drugstore.)

When Blanche didn't arrive home that night as expected, her aunt, Mrs. Noble, went to the church's evening prayer meeting at 7 p.m., figuring she'd find her there. Mrs. Noble didn't see Blanche, but Durrant approached her and asked if Blanche had come to the meeting with her.

Mrs. Noble waited a few days. Then, when Blanche still hadn't returned home, she contacted the police.

Durrant stopped by Mrs. Noble's home a few days later. He said the word around the medical school was that Blanche had been kidnapped and was working in a house of ill-repute. Durrant offered to look for her. He told Henry Partridge, a fellow medical student, the same basic story. "Blanche had gone among the fallen women," said Durrant. "She was easily led astray."[15]

And then, sometime between April 4 and 10, someone tried to sell one of Blanche's rings to a pawn shop. Finally, on April 13, Mrs. Noble received a package. Inside it, she found the three rings Blanche was wearing when she disappeared wrapped in a copy of the *San Francisco Examiner*.[16]

After that, the prosecutor briefly mentioned Minnie Williams's murder, but only as it touched on Blanche Lamont's case.

A group of ladies visited the church early on April 13 to decorate for the Easter celebration. Unfortunately, they discovered Minnie's half-naked, mutilated body when they entered the library.

Detectives made a thorough search of the church, looking for clues. The following day, they found Blanche Lamont's body in the church belfry.

"She lay unclothed upon her back, her feet together, her hands crossed over her bosom, and her head supported by two blocks of wood in the manner in which medical students are accustomed to lay out dead bodies."

The coroner's examination showed she was strangled. There were five fingernail incisions on one side of her neck and seven on the other. She was completely naked. The body was black and beginning to show signs of decomposition.[17]

After the prosecutor finished summarizing the case, the jury visited the Emanuel Baptist Church to examine the crime scene in detail.

A few days later, the prosecution brought in a manikin dressed in the tattered clothes Blanche wore the night she died.

The defense had relied heavily on Dr. Barrett's guess that the girl weighed between 140 and 160 pounds. That would have made it nearly impossible for a man of Durrant's small stature to lug the body upstairs to the belfry.

However, how the clothes fit the manikin showed the girl was much lighter than suggested. The prosecutor questioned Maud Lamont about her sister's weight. She said they weighed themselves at Charlton & Malin's Grocery Store when Blanche arrived from Montana the previous September. Blanched tipped the scale at 115 pounds. Maud guessed her sister had gained five or ten pounds in the intervening months.[18] So, she weighed no more than 125 pounds.

Finally, Defense attorney Eugene Deuprey pulled out his trump card. He accused Reverend J. George Gibson, Emanuel Baptist Church's pastor, of murdering the two women.

He suggested the pastor used the chisel found in his toolbox to pry open the door to the belfry so that he could hide the body. It was no coincidence that the marks from that chisel "exactly fit those marks on the belfry door." Another thing he found suspicious was that Pastor Gibson's writing was similar to that on the newspapers Tryphena Noble received when her niece's rings were returned.[19]

It was a good try, but Chief Isaac Lees quickly proved that Gibson had nothing to do with the girl's murders.

The trial closed a month later, on November 1. The jury took less than thirty minutes before returning a guilty verdict against Theodore Durrant. A month later, Judge Murphy sentenced him to death by hanging.[20]

Theodore Durrant's Final Days

Durrant appealed and wound up being tried four times. Each time, the verdict was death by hanging. Finally, his execution was set for January 7, 1898.

Durrant remained calm and relaxed as he realized he was out of options. He was all questions the week before he was scheduled to die.

What could he expect? What kind of bindings would they use? How long was the walk from his cell to the scaffold?

And more importantly, what would be done with his body? Durrant didn't want anyone to examine his body or perform an autopsy. Instead, he preferred to be placed in the coffin wearing his death cap. He didn't want anyone to see his face except his parents.

Finally, he made it clear that he thought it was all a giant conspiracy. The police, the courts, and the newspapers were all against him. They were more interested in seeing someone hung for the crime than seeing justice rendered.[21]

E. H. Hamilton covered the hanging for the *San Francisco Examiner*.

"Father Lagan administered the rites of the church. The straps were fastened on the prisoner's arms. The mother was led away to the matron's room." Durrant's father sat with the doctors in front of the scaffold, honoring his son's final wishes.

Theodore Durrant walked into the death chamber, glancing casually at the dangling rope. His face was pale, but he showed no sign of fear or any emotion. Instead, his step was steady as he climbed the stairs to the trap.

Behind him, three men sat in a small, boxed-in area. Each man had a rope he was to cut. That way, they could walk away with a clear conscience, not knowing who sprung the trap and sent the prisoner plunging to his death.

Amos Lunt, the hangman, fastened the noose around Durrant's neck, carefully drawing the knot close under the left ear.

"Don't tighten the rope until I'm ready," said Durrant.

Then Durrant turned to the audience and had his final say. "I have no animosity against anyone. But for those who persecuted me and have hounded me to my grave, innocent as I am—I forgive them all.

"I appear before the whole world as an innocent boy to proclaim my innocence for the last time."

When Durrant finished speaking, the knot was drawn tight over his ear. The black cap came down over his head. A moment later, the hangman raised his hand.

Theodore Durrant's body shot through the trap. His neck snapped, and he died almost immediately. Ten minutes later, the doctors pronounced Theodore Durrant dead.

His body was cut down and placed in the waiting coffin.

Amos Lunt wiped a tear from his eye. "He died the bravest of any man I've ever seen," said Lunt. "I have never seen such nerve, and never do I expect to see anything like it again."[22]

The *Demon of the Belfry* was dead.

Murder on Suisun Road (1896)

Elizabeth Dickinson, Addie Wilson, and W. J. Miller were arrested in late January 1899 for the 1896 murder of Daniel H. Wilson in Suisun, California.

Detectives believed Miller was the killer, and his aged mother, Elizabeth Dickinson, and his sister, Addie Wilson, assisted or conspired with him to kill Wilson.

The *San Francisco Call* didn't have anything good to say about them.

They reported Elizabeth Dickinson "is counted as a dangerous woman who will shoot as quickly as a man. The daughter, hard-visaged, scowling, sullen with wickedly gleaming eyes, showed absolutely no emotion. If she felt any fear, she gave no sign. The son, ill-looking, uncouth, bitter in his rage, loudly proclaimed himself guiltless, and he defied anyone to prove him otherwise."[23]

W. J Miller suffered from an "affliction of the eyes that gives him a sinister expression." He paced the corridors of the Fairfield County Jail like a "caged animal."[24]

The reporter for the *Call* had no doubt Miller was a killer. He looked the part, as did his sister, Addie Wilson. Her eyes gleamed with hate while she "sat silently in her cell like an insane beast." And all the while, Elizabeth Dickinson cried, trying to understand what had happened.

All three came from poor families and had lived most of their lives as hermits, secluded in their solitary farmhouse on Suisun Road. They didn't understand how to deal with people.

Miller told detectives he was at home in Vallejo when Daniel Wilson was murdered. He spent the day with his neighbor Maggie Sheehan and her daughters. When she told him about Wilson's murder, he decided to rent a buggy to go up there, so he was nowhere near Suisun Road when the murder occurred.

Besides, what was his motive? He had nothing to gain from killing Wilson. Not that he cared much for "old man" Wilson. "He probably deserved his fate."[25]

And yes, he and his sister accused each other of killing Wilson. But those accusations were made in the heat of anger. They were mad and would have said anything to hurt each other.

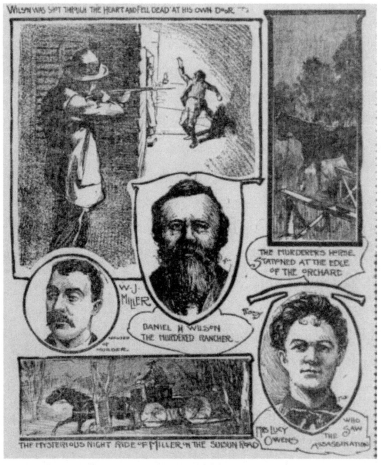

The San Francisco Call printed this illustration of Daniel Wilson's murder and the key players in the case. (San Francisco Call. April 20, 1899.)

The facts were:

Daniel Wilson was shot to death outside the door of his home on October 9, 1896. Addie Wilson, his former wife, and her mother, Elizabeth Dickinson, lived on a ranch just over a mile away from Wilson's place. W. J.

Miller lived in Vallejo, about an hour and a half away, round trip.

Wilson rode into town earlier in the day to settle accounts on his almond crop. He returned home at about 7 p.m. and sat down to dinner. A few minutes later, something struck the door. Again and again.

After the second thud, a scantily clad Lucy Owens walked toward the door, saying she was going to get some water. Wilson stopped her and said he'd handle it with his shotgun if it happened again.

Lucy continued to the door and disappeared into the dark. Unknown to her, Wilson followed her out.

Lucy filled a pitcher with water and returned to the house. A moment later, she heard someone knock on the door. Then Wilson screamed, "Don't lock me out, Lucy."

She heard the report of a rifle and saw a flash of light as she opened the door. Daniel Wilson fell dead at her feet with a bullet through his head.

And even though it was dark out, Lucy swore she saw a man and a woman hurrying away.

The following morning, searchers followed the killer's tracks to a little bridge on the ranch's edge. They figured a horse had been tied to the bridge, waiting for his owner's return. From there, the killer disappeared.

Lucy Owens and her brother, John Hanchard, were held as suspects but quickly released for lack of evidence. Detectives suspected W. J. Miller, Addie Wilson, Mrs. Dickinson, and Mr. McEwen (Elizabeth Dickinson's lover), might have had a hand in Wilson's death. But, as with Lucy Owens, they didn't have any evidence to press a case

Lucy Owens was in a mood, anyway. She'd just learned it was her last day working at Wilson's place. The old man had coaxed Virgie O'Brien, his former housekeeper, back by promising to deed his property to her.

Addie Wilson was just as surprised as Lucy Owens. Her son had brought her news of the impending transfer a week before her former husband's murder. She had expected her children would inherit the property, providing a home for her. Now, her hopes were gone.

Sheriff George Savage spent over two years piecing the clues together. The only problem was that W. J. Miller had disappeared immediately after his release in 1896. Savage finally found Miller working as a switchman between Porta Costa and Benicia.

"I know who killed Wilson," Miller told Sheriff Savage, "and I can hang him."[26] But, of course, he had no idea. He was just blowing off steam.

Sheriff Savage figured Daniel Wilson was murdered to keep him from deeding his property to his new girlfriend and mistress, Virgie O'Brien. She had started as his housekeeper and worked her way into his heart and pocketbook.

O'Brien eventually left Wilson, so he hired Lucy Owens as his new housekeeper. On the night Wilson was shot, Owens was in the house with her niece, Ada Rice.

The San Francisco Call described Wilson as "an ignorant, rough, uncouth old farmer." He didn't give a damn what people thought. As long as he could care for himself and pay his bills, he would live with his mistress. Let the world be damned.[27]

He divorced his wife in 1893. After that, Addie Wilson went to live with her mom on H. W. McEwen's ranch.

Sheriff Savage thoroughly searched H. W. McEwen's place after he arrested Dickinson, Wilson, and Miller. At first, it looked like a bust. He couldn't find any evidence to tie them to the murder. Then he checked the shotgun pellets. The lead pellets used to kill Wilson were made from a strange mold that investigators had not seen before. And then, when they searched McEwen's ranch, they found a matching mold.

Detectives suspected Addie Wilson assisted her brother-in-law in killing her former husband. But unfortunately, they didn't have enough evidence to bring the case to trial. (San Francisco Call. January 11, 1899.)

McEwen admitted the gun that fired the shots that killed Wilson was his. After that, he just shrugged his shoulders. Possessing the murder weapon didn't mean he pulled the trigger.

Sheriff George Savage did some more investigating. He discovered Addie Wilson's son, Daniel Wilson, Jr., had told her about the change in her ex-husband's will a week before the shooting. Shortly after that, McEwen and Mrs. Dickinson went to Vallejo to talk with W. J. Miller. That tied the conspirators together.

Then the sheriff dug a little deeper. He found a witness who could place Miller and McEwen at the Wilson ranch the Sunday before the murder. He believed they were exploring the lay of the land, planning their crime.

He also had a witness who would testify that Dickinson and McEwen were at Miller's Vallejo home at 2 a.m. on October 9. The San Francisco Call suggested it "wasn't difficult to draw the inference that some conference of moment had been in progress in the Miller household that night."[28]

It was little more than circumstantial evidence, but the paper took it as proof of a conspiracy.

The sheriff learned that Miller rented a horse and buggy from Callender Stables in Vallejo at 5:30 on the afternoon of the murder. And then, at 6 p.m., a woman saw him pass her house on Suisun Road, going toward the Wilson ranch.

Miller returned the horse and buggy at 6 a.m. the following morning. Investigators can only speculate on his whereabouts and what he did in the intervening twelve hours.

What the sheriff did know was the shoe imprints found in the soft ground around Wilson's ranch matched Miller's shoes. And they were a size 7—the same size worn by Miller.

Miller insisted he was home watching his children when he was supposed to have rented the team. Mrs. Sheehan and her daughters backed him up.

The sheriff didn't believe her, but...he still couldn't prove Miller pulled the trigger.

Addie Wilson's daughter told Sheriff Savage her mom was restless and uneasy the entire night. She paced around the house nervously. And then, finally, she went outside and started walking toward the Wilson ranch. When she heard the gunshot, she returned home and threw herself on the bed, fully clothed.

That made it seem like she knew what was going on.

And then, just when it seemed authorities had the case against W. J. Miller sewed up, they arrested John L. Owens, Lucy Owens's husband.[29]

Nearly four years after Daniel Wilson's murder, the authorities arrested John Owens. He confessed to killing "old man" Owens in hopes his wife, Lucy Owens (Wilson's housekeeper), would return home. (San Francisco Call. April 21, 1900.)

The sheriff figured Owens left his home in Healdsburg early on October 8, carrying a double-barreled shotgun of no. 10 bore. When detectives searched Owens's house, they found a bullet mold that molded the same size bullets used to kill Wilson.[30]

After that, it was just a matter of sweating a confession out of him. It didn't take long to break him. John Owens made a full confession on April 20, 1900.

He said his wife left him to care for their three small children. "I worked hard to feed and clothe them, and my failure to do so properly made me brood over the affair. I worried myself almost to death. I wrote to my wife to come back, but she refused. I also wrote to Wilson. He never answered my letter. So, I made up my mind to kill Wilson."[31]

Owens said he drove his buggy within a mile of Wilson's house. Then he walked toward the house and waited for Wilson to come out. When he did, Owens pulled the trigger and shot him.

His wife didn't know anything about it.

The sad part was that Lucy Owens had received her notice and was leaving Wilson's home the next day. If John Owens had waited another day or two, his wife would have been back home with him.

On July 12, 1900, Judge A. J. Buckles sentenced John Owens to life in Folsom Prison. It was the best he could do since Owens had agreed to plead guilty if the prosecution promised he would not receive the death penalty.[32]

Owens was quiet after his conviction. Finally, he told deputies, "I made a mistake and will have to take my medicine."[33]

The San Francisco Troll (1897)

Mary Clute was brutally murdered in her home at 803 Guerrero Street on December 15, 1897. However, the police got an unexpected break the following morning when sixty-five-old Albert Hoff (real name Albert Vereneseneckockhoff) walked into the police station and told Chief Isaac Lees he had some explaining to do.

If Albert Hoff killed Mary Clute, he definitely wasn't the sharpest stone in the shed. He walked into the police station and told the chief he was in the house moments before the murder occurred. And then, as he told his story, he raised his arms, displaying a fresh bruise on his left palm. After that, detectives couldn't help noticing the bloodstains on his pants.

Hoff's words might have said he wasn't the killer, but everything detectives saw told them he was their man.

Hoff said he learned of the murder when someone brought a newspaper into his friend Thomas Hannon's place.

"Let me see that paper," he said. "I want to read that story."

After that, he explained his predicament to Hannon. He was in the house with the victim the previous day. He was supposed to return today to do some work for her.

"I suppose I will get into trouble for this," said Hoff. "I do not know what I ought to do. I think I shall go to the city hall and tell the chief of police all I know."[34]

And that's what he did. Hoff went to the police station to say he was the man witnesses saw leaving the house, but not the killer.

He was dirty, shifty, and nervous as detectives questioned him. Chief Lees took an immediate disliking to Albert Hoff.

"He is hideous," the chief told reporters. "He has a little head flat as a snake's, marked by strange depressions like the sinking sides of an old orange. It is partly covered with lifeless hair and set on so mean a throat that it seems to squat unsupported between his shoulders and throws a length of rusty beard flat as a doormat on his chest. His small pale eyes shrink under a shelving brow, his nose sunken, boneless, at the bridge, rises into a small sharp snout. The rough hair on his lips sprouts outward and betrays a brutal line beneath and above the beard on either side. His cheeks hang out and loose in dreadful sacks. It is the face of a troll."[35]

The papers didn't have anything good to say about 65-year-old Albert Hoff. Instead, he was described as a dirty, unkempt troll. Mrs. L. A Legg just shook her head at the coroner's inquest, saying, "I thought what a bad-looking fellow he was. His eyes seemed so mean and ugly." (San Francisco Examiner. December 17, 1897.)

While Hoff talked, detectives noted a fresh scar on his left hand and blood smears on his pants. Hoff explained the bruise, saying he cut it on a carpet tack at Mrs. Clute's house. Then when questioned further, he changed his story and said he tore it up lugging a heavy carpet, but the detectives knew better. A carpet tack couldn't have caused such an injury. It would have taken a much heavier instrument, similar to the bloody railroad coupling pin found near Clute's body, to make such a bruise.

A little investigation proved that Albert Hoff likely owned the murder weapon. Additionally, he was reportedly drunk and in an "ugly mood" on the day of the killing.[36]

That was enough for Chief Lees to charge Albert Hoff with Mary Clute's murder. Now the real work began—uncovering the missing details that would put Hoff on the gallows.

The victim's husband, Edward Clute, a traveling salesman for the Price Baking Powder Company, was away at the time. As a result, Mrs. Clute was taking care of their move on her own.

Albert Hoff had previously helped the couple with some chores, so Mrs. Clute asked him to come and see her. When Hoff arrived at the house, she explained she wanted help moving a few items, hanging some pictures, and laying the carpet.

Hoff stopped by Clute's house the following day. He was "a short, chunky, middle-aged German, with a heavy, ill-kept beard and a coarse, brutal face, which took on a fiendish expression when angered."[37]

Unfortunately, before Hoff arrived, Mary Clute found out the carpet store wouldn't sell her the matting for her rugs unless they installed them, so she had to let them do it.

When Hoff showed up, Mary explained her predicament but said she'd still have some pictures for him to hang the next day. But when Hoff showed up, Mary wasn't ready for him. The movers had delayed moving her stuff, so he had to return.

Hoff was visibly upset, slightly intoxicated, and smelled of whiskey. Mary left him and went to her new place to check on a few things. Unknown to her, Hoff followed her.

He walked into her new apartment as Joseph Foley was laying carpet and wandered about aimlessly, poking his nose into things. Foley finished working and left just before 5 p.m.

A few minutes later, Mary's downstairs neighbor, George Legg, heard a series of piercing screams followed by a loud thud.

His daughter-in-law, Mrs. L. A. Legg, ran upstairs. She saw a man hurrying down the hallway toward the back stairs and watched him disappear with a bag of tools. Then, when George Legg hollered at him to come back, the man stepped up his pace and hurried away.

Mary Clute, age 45, came to America from London, England. Her parents had died a year ago, leaving her nearly $50,000 in cash and property. (San Francisco Examiner. December 16, 1897.)

After watching Hoff walk away, they went back upstairs to investigate. Mary Clute's lifeless body lay in a back bedroom. There was blood everywhere. Her face was beaten beyond recognition, and her skull was fractured in numerous places. And next to the body, they found a blood-spattered railroad coupling pin.

What puzzled the police was the killer's motive. Mary Clute was wearing several expensive pieces of jewelry, including a gold watch, and she had $56 in her bag, so the attack didn't appear to be a robbery.

The police charged Albert Hoff with Mary Clute's murder on March 15, 1897.

Hoff told Chief Lees he was born in Walsingen, Germany. He came to America when he was nineteen and wandered around the country a bit. He lived in Baltimore for a short time. From there, he went to Cincinnati, where he worked as a cashier and bartender at a billiard parlor for three years.

He spent six weeks in St. Louis and moved to New Orleans, Houston, Texas, and Denver, Colorado.

He found himself in San Francisco in the early 1870s, traveled a little more, and then returned to this city.[38]

When police checked Hoff out, they discovered he had an unblemished record in the city. He'd worked in hundreds of homes around San Francisco. People said he was "kind and considerate," good with children, and did a great job.[39]

Albert Hoff had done some repair work for Mary Clute in the past, so she felt comfortable inviting him into her home. Unfortunately, something inside Hoff snapped, and he bludgeoned her to death with a railroad coupling pin. (San Francisco Examiner. December 16, 1897.)

Hoff did, however, have a dark side. He was an anarchist and regularly attended meetings of the local anarchist and socialist societies.

And he didn't have a high opinion of women. He thought they were all "immoral," wrote the *San Francisco Examiner*. He spoke foully about them whenever possible and went to great lengths to disgust his listeners.[40]

The police established beyond a doubt that Albert Hoff was in Mary Clute's home at 803 Guerrero Street when she was killed. "If he did not commit the crime," said Chief Lees, "he was in the house when Mrs. Clute was beaten to death."[41]

Hoff had a ready explanation for who might have done it. He told detectives that after Foley left, the doorbell rang, and Mary Clute let a well-dressed man in. Hoff wasn't sure what had happened after that. The man just disappeared, but not through the front door. And detectives knew he couldn't have escaped through the back door because George Legg had kept a close watch on it, and no one came in or out.

Additional evidence came out at the coroner's inquest, held a few days after Mary Clute's murder.

The police picked up Joseph Foley at a barber shop about an hour after Clute's murder, but he wasn't much help.

"I know nothing whatever about this murder," said Foley. "As I left by the front door, I heard footsteps on the back stairway." But he didn't see anyone else in the house except his partner, Henry Jackson, who'd left over a half hour before he did.

The evidence showed that Albert Hoff was the only person who left through the back door. George Legg and Mrs. L. A. Legg watched him walk out after they heard Mary Clute's dying screams. And Hoff's testimony verified it was him.

Mrs. Legg ran up the stairs moments after her father-in-law heard the woman scream and the body fall to the floor. She saw a man, similar to Hoff, rushing toward the stairs.

"She heard his heavy steps on the rear stairs. She heard him unlock the door that led to the yard. Then with her father-in-law, George Legg, she opened the front door and stepped out on the porch. A moment later, Hoff ran rather than walked out of the passage and started up Liberty Street." They called out to him, but he wouldn't stop.[42]

Mrs. Legg had no doubt Hoff was the man she saw.

Perhaps the most incriminating evidence was the shoulder end of the coupling pin fit into the wound on the palm of Hoff's hand.[43]

Hoff swore he didn't own a coupling pin or carry an iron bar in his tool bag. He had no use for such an instrument. However, the police quickly proved he was lying.

J. G. Zimblemann testified at the coroner's inquest on December 22. He said he saw the coupling pin in Hoff's tool bag.

"I was looking for a nail. At the same time, I was looking around and saw a coupling pin in the bag. I pushed it to one side. I thought to myself that is a ——— of a tool for an upholster."[44]

When Edward Clute heard those words, he leaned forward over Hoff and whispered, "No matter what the judges and jurors may say, I know you are the murderer of my wife."[45]

And then, Mayer May, testified that Hoff carried a coupling pin in his tool bag several years back when he worked for him. When he asked Hoff how he used it to lay carpet, Hoff smiled and said he'd find a use. May assumed he carried it for protection.[46]

After that, no one questioned that the coupling pin belonged to Hoff.

Hoff's only hope was that the jury would believe his friend, Robert Goepel's testimony. Goepel said he saw Hoff in the Cosy Saloon on Van Ness Avenue and Turk street sometime between 4 and 5 p.m.

However, Chief Lees brushed Goepel's testimony off as inconsequential, saying he was "so stupid that he hardly knows he is alive." Besides, he was always drunk.[47]

And then, Dr. H. Kugler hinted that Mary Clute had been sexually assaulted before she was murdered, but he couldn't say for sure. Too much time had passed for the examination to prove conclusive. However, "the indications were that a most horrible crime had been added to that of murder."[48]

After hearing all the evidence, the coroner's jury returned a verdict charging Hoff with the murder of Mary Clute.

Albert Hoff's trial opened on March 15, 1898, and closed on April 2. The jury deliberated for less than a half hour before returning a guilty verdict.

Hoff seemed surprised by the decision.

"I don't know what I shall do now," he said. "I suppose I must hang."

Then he took a deep breath and continued. "You may tell the people of San Francisco that old Hoff is as innocent as an unborn babe."[49]

His attorneys appealed the decision, and the Supreme Court granted Hoff a new trial, saying the judge "discussed too many facts instead of the law."[50]

Albert Hoff pretty much convicted himself. He walked into the police station with a fresh bruise on his palm and bloodstains on his pants and told Chief Isaac Lees he was in the house with Mary Clute just moments before she was killed. (San Francisco Examiner. December 27, 1897.)

The jury in the second trial in December 1900 found Hoff guilty of first-degree murder. He received a life sentence this time rather than death by hanging.[51]

Cordelia Botkin, The San Francisco Borgia (1898)

Mary Elizabeth Dunning received a box of chocolates in the mail in early August 1898. Inside the box, she found a short note. "With love to yourself and baby. Mrs. C."

She ate a few pieces and shared some with her sister, her children, and a few friends. Three days later, Elizabeth Dunning and her sister, Ida Deane, died.

Several guests got sick but quickly recovered. Another guest, Josephine Bateman, tasted a piece of the candy, then spit it out—something about the taste bothered her. Afterward, she wiped a white powder out of her mouth.[52] After that, she didn't give it another thought until her friends died.

The dead women's father, ex-congressman John P. Pennington, was suspicious and requested an investigation into the deaths. Pennington wasn't sure but thought the candy might be to blame—maybe a jealous woman in San Francisco poisoned his daughters, although he didn't know why.

Dr. L. A. Bishop, who cared for the two women during their illness, believed the cause of death was poisoning. He agreed with Pennington that the candy was the likely source. Detectives sent samples to the lab at the Pennsylvania Railroad Company and the Associated Press for testing.

After testing the samples, Dr. Theodore Wolf was sure the candy caused the women's death. "The candy contained a very large quantity of arsenic," said Wolf. "I found pieces of arsenic as large as peas."

He wasn't sure, but the poison might have been *Rough On Rats*, a popular rodent killer. Each piece of candy contained between ten to twelve grains of arsenic, enough to kill four people.[53]

And yet, autopsies weren't conducted for some reason, so that that arsenic poisoning couldn't be proven.

Elizabeth Dunning's husband, John P. Dunning, a war correspondent for the Associated Press, was covering the Spanish American War in Cuba and Porto Rico when his wife died. The previous month he'd sent Elizabeth a letter describing the actions he was in, parts of which were quoted in the local paper.

"I was in the fight of the Rough Riders within six or eight miles of Santiago," wrote Dunning, "in which about twenty of our men were killed and many wounded. It certainly was hot for an hour, but I got out with whole skin."

Mary Elizabeth Dunning died from arsenic poisoning after eating chocolates she received in the mail. (San Francisco Call. August 29, 1898.)

Dunning closed the letter, saying it seemed like a "thousand Spanish bullets whispered around my ears."[54]

In late August, when he returned from Cuba, John Dunning identified Cordelia Botkin as the author of two anonymous letters sent to his wife. He said she received them about a year ago. "The contents are such that they should not be made public."[55]

He had received 300 or 400 letters from Mrs. Botkin and knew her writing well.

After Dunning identified Cordelia Botkin as the sender of the chocolates, the action moved to San Francisco, California.

The problem was that California law was a bit tricky on extradition. The state's constitution prohibited the extradition of prisoners unless proof of flight from the state demanding extradition was supplied. Cordelia Botkin had never been to Delaware. Therefore, her flight was impossible. So legally, Cordelia Botkin could not be extradited to stand trial in Delaware.[56]

At the same time, California law made it clear she couldn't be tried for a crime that occurred out of state or partially out of state. That provided a conundrum for law enforcement officials.

And yet, Cordelia Botkin was in jail, charged with murder for a crime the state couldn't legally try her. The police understood the unique circumstances of the case.

Their goal was to hold her long enough for evidence to arrive from Delaware. Then they could determine their next step.

John P. Dunning was a war correspondent for the Associated Press, covering the Spanish American War in Cuba and Porto Rico when his wife was killed. (San Francisco Call. August 28, 1898.)

Detective Bernard. J. McVey was expected shortly. He was bringing the candy box, samples of the candy, and the wrapper it arrived in—the San Francisco police and district attorney needed to build a case from those scraps.

The box itself was a standard candy box used by every candy seller in the country. It was 7 1/2 inches long, 3 3/4 inches wide, and 1 7/8 inches deep. The buff wrapper it was enclosed in was addressed to Mrs. John P. Dunning, Dover, Delaware. And inside was a short note. "With love to yourself and baby. Mrs. C."

However, "the candy itself plainly showed the devilish work of the assassin," wrote the *San Francisco Call.* "A casual observer might say that the surface of the chocolate creams had been broken in the long journey across the continent. A closer examination shows that the candies have been drawn out to receive the poison within and then, by a slight pressure, been contracted to the original size. In the operation, the outer surface has been broken. The box is still almost full of candy."[57]

The postmark showed the package was mailed on August 4. J. E. Fenenessee, a clerk at the Philadelphia Shoe Store, saw a woman drop a package "about the size of a four-bit box of candy" into the mail drop at the Tiburon Ferry entrance that afternoon. He was positive the time was 5:45 p.m. because the incident occurred just as he boarded the ferry to Oakland.

The case quickly became headline news across the country.

On August 30, the *San Francisco Call* printed a letter from Cordelia Botkin explaining her position. She had never met Mrs. Dunning and never had any feelings against her. She was not and never had been in love with John P. Dunning.

Cordelia Botkin insisted that she was "incapable of committing such a crime."[58]

However, that didn't stop detectives from building their case. They believed the candy was sold to Mrs. Botkin by Frank Gattrell, a clerk at the Wave Candy Store in Stockton, California.

The following week it was learned the candy was purchased at George Haas's establishment on Market Street. The salesgirl, Emma Herber, did not think she could identify the buyer. They sold at least fifty such boxes a week. So, remembering one person would be next to impossible.[59]

The police also learned that the lace handkerchief packed inside the candy box was purchased from the City of Paris store in San Francisco. It was sold for 25 cents on August 4. No one could say whether Cordelia Botkin bought it, but she was known to be a frequent shopper at the store and had cashed a money order there that day.

Haas's store was just two blocks from the City of Paris, making it a good bet the poison was purchased in the same neighborhood. So, detectives began searching drugstores to see if anyone remembered selling arsenic that day.

The police also knew that Cordelia Botkin had a keen interest in poisons and their effects. A few days before the candies were mailed, she had a long discussion with her friend, Almira Ruouf.[60]

Ruouf said Mrs. Botkin took sick while visiting her in late July. She heard her asking the doctor all sorts of questions about poisons. Mrs. Botkin wondered "what the effects of different poisons were upon the human system." Mrs. Ruouf told the doctor not to answer because she thought Mrs. Botkin was contemplating suicide.

Ruouf remembered Mrs. Botkin asking about strychnine. The doctor was against using it for suicide because of the "excruciating pain it caused." After that, they talked about arsenic and chloroform. The doctor said they "were easier and did not work so quickly."[61]

Finally, Chief Lees based his initial case on the note in the chocolate box. The author put "with love to yourself and baby" in quotation marks. Cordelia Botkin used quotation marks in all her writing.

The quotation marks in her writing, the note enclosed with the candy, and the letters to Elizabeth Dunning convinced the grand jury that Cordelia Botkin was somehow involved in the murder of the two women.

Cordelia Botkin, in what the papers said, was her favorite pose. She was always posing as if she was the star of some great show. (Los Angeles Herald, August 30, 1898.)

On August 3, detectives learned that Frank Grey, a clerk at the Owl Drug Store on Market Street, sold two ounces of arsenic to Cordelia Botkin on June 1. She said she was going to bleach some straw hats. He suggested a less dangerous chemical, but Mrs. Botkin said she had used it before and understood it.[62]

Chief Lees believed the discovery that Cordelia Botkin had purchased arsenic proved the case against her. However, Mr. Blaisdell, the manager of the Owl Drug Store, figured it proved the opposite.

"If the crystalline form was used, as is claimed, then the Owl Drug Store did not sell it to Mrs. Botkin. She purchased the fine white powder," said the druggist. "It cannot be changed into crystals or small pieces."[63] In other words, the police were barking up the wrong tree.

And then, a few days later, there was news from Delaware that the two women were poisoned with powdered and crystalline arsenic. Delaware State Chemist Thomas R. Wolf said, "the poison was worked in through the cream of the chocolates and was in a powdered form."[64] He also founds chunks of arsenic in some of the other candies.

The rumor was that Cordelia Botkin had been having an affair with John P. Dunning for at least three years. She had picked him up out of the gutter and reinvigorated him spiritually, financially, and sexually. And then, not long before Elizabeth Dunning was murdered, her husband told Cordelia Botkin he intended to move back to New York with his wife when the war ended.

The San Francisco Call printed this drawing of Cordelia Botkin buying and mailing the candy that killed Mary Elizabeth Dunning and her sister, Ida Deane. (San Francisco Call. December 23, 1898.)

The news came as a devastating blow to Cordelia Botkin. She was estranged from her husband and had not lived with him for two years.

Meanwhile, the California Supreme Court refused Delaware's writ of habeas corpus. As a result, Cordelia Botkin was not extradited to Delaware to stand trial.

That left California authorities unsure of their next move. As a result, prosecutors found themselves treading uncharted territory as they built their case against her.

The Supreme Court had ruled that Cordelia Botkin could not be extradited to Delaware under California law. She could only be tried there if she voluntarily went to that state. So finally, the prosecutors decided to try her in San Francisco, but no one was sure they had the legal right to do so.

Cordelia Botkin's trial started on December 5, 1898, and was filled with many exciting twists and turns.

In a surprise move, Judge Carroll Cook seemed to take offense at John Dunning's many affairs. When Dunning refused to name all the women he had slept with while in San Francisco, Judge Cook locked him up in the county jail. The *San Francisco Call* said Dunning "confessed a moral obliquity that stamps him as despicable." Nevertheless, he seemed to take considerable pride in his many conquests.[65]

Dunning admitted his affair with Cordelia Botkin. However, the paper didn't feel it necessary to go into the details of the relationship. Instead, they satisfied themselves, saying, "it was an unvarnished, revolting story of unadorned vice."

And then, when he finished telling his story, Dunning said he had told Botkin his wife was "passionately fond of candy." It was as good as an admission that he put the gun in her hand. All that was left was to pull the trigger.[66]

Dunning finally admitted to being intimate with many women in the city—maybe six altogether. Some he knew the names of, and some he didn't. It didn't matter.

Lizzie Livernash, a reporter for the *San Francisco Examiner*, cozied up to Cordelia Botkin shortly after she became a suspect in the murders. And then, Livernash spilled her guts on the witness stand, detailing the ups and downs of Botkin's affair with Dunning. The "orgies at 927 Geary Street were described in merciless detail."[67]

"Mrs. Botkin loved the pleasures of the world," said Livernash. She "would not let anything stand in her way to gratify her desires, not even the divorce court."

Botkin told Livernash, "she was an English woman and believed in living as they did." They had husbands who "provide them with all comforts, and they also have lovers with whom they lived in intimacy."[68]

When the affair started, John Dunning was little more than an impoverished wreck. He was a drunken, mental case who spent his time and what little money he had at the racetrack.

Cordelia Botkin housed and fed Dunning. Several times, she kept him from taking his life. And he repaid her by deciding to return to his wife at the war's end.

Livernash painted a picture of Cordelia Botkin as a woman who would do anything for pleasure. Then, finally, Botkin told her that "it would have been far better to let the man die and spare the mother for her child."[69]

Perhaps, it was a confession of guilt. Livernash wasn't sure.

And, of course, Cordelia Botkin wasn't the only cheater in her marriage. Her husband had been enjoying a long-running affair with Clara Arbogast.

When Mrs. Botkin was arrested, Welcome A. Botkin agreed to cover his wife's legal expenses if Mrs. Arbogast's name didn't become entangled in the case. But, when it did, he cut off all support.

When she was on the witness stand, Cordelia Botkin didn't accuse Arbogast of the crime, not directly, anyway. However, she did suggest that the prosecution should investigate the life of Clara Argobast. "If they did, they would find her motive for disposing of Mrs. Dunning was far stronger than any alleged one they could have attributed to me."[70]

On December 30, 1898, the jury found Cordelia Botkin guilty of murder in the first degree and sentenced her to life in prison.[71]

Her lawyers quickly appealed the case.

Finally, in March 1901, the California Supreme Court granted Cordelia Botkin a new trial based on errors in the charge to the jury. But unfortunately, they also sustained the lower court's jurisdiction in the case. That came as a fatal blow to Botkin's attorneys, who expected the court would deny jurisdiction and dismiss the case.[72]

At her second trial in April 1904, the jury found Cordelia Botkin guilty of murder in the first degree and sentenced her to life in prison.[73]

Botkin spent six years in a private cell at the Branch County Jail. And then, in June 1905, the grand jury visited the jail and found her living "in a condition of comfort almost approaching luxury." They thought that was improper for the murderess and ordered her to be treated like the other female prisoners.

The *San Francisco Examiner* said Botkin had fixed her room like a comfortable apartment. She had nice furniture, painted walls, a bookcase, and fresh flowers in her window.

"Henceforth, Mrs. Botkin must fare no better and no worse than the other female inmates of the jail," ordered the grand jury.[74]

Cordelia Botkin died at San Quentin in March 1910 after spending twelve years in prison. She was "broken in health and spirits—a pitiable wreck."[75]

Midnight Murder at Hubbard House (1898)

Admit it. Who isn't afraid of strange sounds in the dark of night?

Lizzie Riley (Spanish Lizzie) awoke to a "scuffling noise." After a while, the noise "gave way to a peculiar scraping sound like a spool of cotton running over the floor." It might have lasted twenty minutes, then a door opened and slammed shut. Afterward, she heard the creak of footsteps as they raced down the stairs and out to the street.[76]

Lizzie tried her neighbor's door but didn't get an answer, so she roused Alphonse Prieur, the night clerk. He woke up Joseph Lochner, another boarder in the house.

Prieur opened Sadie's door with his passkey, then fumbled with a match as he tried to ignite the gaslight. Joseph Lochner rushed forward and felt for the woman's form. Her face was warm, but her hands felt cold and icy.

His hands crawled over her face. Something was wrapped tightly around her neck. Lochner untied it just as the lights came on.

Sadie's face showed signs of a struggle. She had fingernail marks on the left side of her face, just below the ear, and the right side of her nose. That one drew blood. She had two bruises on her knee and a red mark on her throat.

Sadie Carpenter, and a look inside her room, the way it looked on the night she died. (San Francisco Call. July 18, 1898)

Papers found in Sadie's room said her maiden name was Anderson. She married Mark J. Simpson on February 28, 1884. She divorced him a year and a half before she died and married Harry S. Carpenter. Now, she was waiting for the court to finalize her divorce.

Investigators also found several letters from Sergeant George Gilligan at Chickamauga, who called himself "her future husband."

After examining the body, Coroner Hawkins said Sadie was malnourished and underdeveloped. She stood 5 feet 6 and weighed just 105 pounds. Dr. Gallagher, the coroner's surgeon, determined the calico cloth tied around Sadie's neck didn't cause her death.

Despite ample evidence to the contrary, Captain Seymour decided the woman committed suicide. He ordered Joseph Lochner held even though his only crime was that he was the last person to see Sadie Carpenter alive.

At the coroner's inquest, Alphonse Prieur said Lochner walked up to the body, untied the cloth around Sadie's neck, then said, Oh, my, I think she is dead." After he learned Sadie was dead, Prieur left Lochner in the room so he could summon a policeman. When he returned, the door was locked, and Lochner was gone.[77]

Lochner said, "he kissed [Sadie] three times. Once for myself, and once for each of her children."[78] When the night clerk left Sadie's room, he went to his room to dress, then hurried off to the Bellevue Saloon to tell the bartender that Sadie was dead. A bricklayer named Thomas Glynn told him, "That's too bad, Joe." He paused, winked at the bartender, then continued, "you will be arrested for it."[79] That set the German off. He complained to the bartender before rushing out the door.

Joseph Lochner in his jail cell at the City Prison. (San Francisco Call. July 21, 1898)

Sadie received several visitors that evening, and the last one before Joseph Lochner was a heavy-set German who stopped at about 9:00 p.m. He left a half-hour later.

Lochner said he left Sadie's room a little after 11 p.m. The spring lock on the door closed as he left. The night clerk woke him at around 1 a.m. and said something was wrong with Sadie.

Spanish Lizzie said Sadie had a premonition she was going to die.

A few days before her murder, Sadie told her that she was afraid someone would strangle her to death, and this wasn't the first time they had threatened her.[80]

For all the talk of strangulation, it turned out strangulation wasn't the cause of death. Instead, the killer smothered Sadie with her pillow or bed clothing. Officials believed the murderer tied the rag around her throat to throw detectives off the track and make them think she had committed suicide.[81]

On the witness stand, Lochner said he did not think he was drunk that night but had drunk two beers and five or six glasses of whiskey.

And there were slight inconsistencies in Lochner's story. At first, he said he could see Sadie's body by the arc light shining through the window. Then, when the police said the light turned off an hour before they entered Sadie's room, Lochner changed his story and said he felt his way to her bed. Lochner also fumbled, talking about the cloth tied around Sadie's neck. He couldn't explain how he untied it in the dark.

The only new evidence came from two jewelry salespeople. George Dolan and Daniel Shea sold Sadie some jewelry a few months back. She told them she feared a German man who lived next door, presumably Joseph Von Lochner.[82] He'd come to the United States from Germany in 1876 and resided at Hubbard House for several years. Rumor had it Lochner was a baron who'd fought in the Franco-German War. And he was the closest person to Sadie Carpenter, sharing an adjoining room with her.

Whatever the police suspected, the coroner's jury ruled that Sadie Carpenter met her death by strangulation through a party unknown. Detectives escorted Lochner back to the City Prison, then released him.

The San Francisco Call ridiculed the police. "Lochner was acquitted as far as it is possible for a man who has never been charged with an offense. Though in custody, he was legally free, yet practically, owing to the devilish police methods of administration, he was on his trial before a jury for the crime of murder."[83]

Butchered on Haight Street (1901)

Bigger cities have always been a haven for fiends and perverts, but the murder of thirteen-year-old Robbie Hislop seemed particularly vicious, even for San Francisco's worst element.

An unknown monster crept through an open window of the Hislop home at 104 ½ Haight Street on May 25, 1901, and butchered young Robbie as he slept. The killer smashed his head with an ax, beating his face beyond recognition. And then, not content with that, he slashed the boy's face over a dozen times, nearly severing his nose.[84]

Halfway down the stairs, detectives found a bloody handprint, as if the killer had stopped for a second to steady himself. Or maybe he started to fall and grabbed the wall to save himself.

Then he ran out the front door, or maybe the back door. The facts remain uncertain.

Nellie Kneeland lived in a flat adjoining the Hislop place. She heard a man running down the back stairs at about 8:30 p.m. Nellie said she imagined the house shaking as if there had been an earthquake, but after she listened a little longer, Nellie figured it was a man racing down the back stairs. She ran to the window but didn't get a good look. However, she was confident "the man was running out of the Hislop flat."[85]

On the other hand, bloodstains on the front steps showed the killer had escaped through the front door. That left the police asking themselves if there were two killers.

Clearly, there were a lot of unknown details detectives needed to uncover.

Robbie Hislop's father ran a furniture store at 341 Hayes Street.

His wife usually walked to the store with her son. And then, after meeting her husband, they returned home together. However, the night he was murdered, Robbie decided to stay home. He made excuses that he was tired and had some schoolwork to finish, so he stayed home alone. Mrs. Hislop tucked Robbie into his bed at 8 p.m., turned off all the lights, then headed to the furniture store, where she helped her husband close up. They stopped for a bite to eat, then headed home.

Thirteen-year-old Robbie Hislop was brutally murdered in his home at 104 ½ Haight Street on May 25, 1901. (San Francisco Call. May 27, 1901)

Mrs. Hislop said she knew something was wrong as they approached the house. They could see that the parlor light was on. And then, as they went inside, they saw Robbie's door was ajar and the light on.

Robbie was still alive but gasping for breath. Blood spatters covered the walls, and blood oozed from the boy's face and head. Robbie died less than an hour later.

Detectives determined that two blows to the base of the skull caused the boy's death. In addition, there were six incised wounds around the right ear, three on the neck, and five on the face—all made with a knife.

Although the knife wounds looked nasty, they were superficial and would not have caused death. In addition, the boy's nose was almost severed, and one hand was cut up as if Robbie had tried to shield himself from his attacker.[86]

Dr. Bacigalupi, the autopsy surgeon, determined that Robbie Hislop was asleep when the attack occurred. He did not see any evidence of a struggle.[87]

What was strange, though, was that someone had ransacked every room in the house, but nothing was taken. That made it seem as if the killer was after something specific.

Dr. T. B. Roche explained that the robbers must have ransacked the house before killing the boy.

"Robert Hislop's murderer must have been covered with blood from head to foot," said Dr. Roche. "Every cut severed an artery. And when an artery is severed, the blood shoots out—sometimes it fairly spouts out, going five and six feet."[88]

Circumstantial evidence pointed to Herman Lukherath, a butcher at a nearby sausage factory. He had boarded at the Hislop home for a few months and had been seen with the boy the previous week. That was all the police needed to arrest him for suspicion of murder.

Lukherath told detectives he left the sausage factory with co-worker Charles Eichorn at about 7 p.m. They had a few drinks at Sheehy's Saloon, where they met his roommate, Harry Smith.[89] They left the saloon a few minutes after 8 p.m. and stopped at L. Samuel's Drugstore on the corner of Ninth and Howard Streets.

Several witnesses backed him up, but that didn't deter Captain Seymour. "I intend to hold him until I'm thoroughly satisfied that he had nothing to do with the murder," said the captain.[90]

His stance didn't make sense because even many detectives working the case felt Lukherath was a dead end. "He seems to be a harmless fellow," one detective told reporters. "Not a man who would commit such a foul crime."

But unfortunately, Herman Lukherath was all they had, and the papers demanded an arrest.

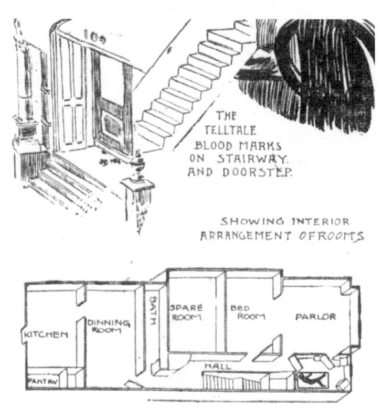

A police sketch shows the home layout where thirteen-year-old Robbie Hislop was murdered. (San Francisco Chronicle. May 27, 1901.)

Lukherath told detectives he was 25 and had come to San Francisco from Norway about three months ago. He stayed at the Winchester Hotel for a week, then took a room at the Hislop house at 104 1/2 Haight Street. He stayed there until March 9, then got a room at 318 Laguna Street, where he roomed with Harry Smith.

The day of the murder went from bad to worse for him. His employer, A. Pflander, the factory manager, discharged him at the end of his shift, paying him his $12 weekly salary. When questioned, Pflander told detectives Lukherath was a lousy worker who drank too much and couldn't follow simple directions.

After work that day, Lukherath went to the saloon across the street with some friends. He stayed there until about 9 p.m., then went to the drugstore to get a salve for Smith's rheumatism. Then, they went home.

Lukherath's roommate, Harry Smith,[91] corroborated the story. "Herman was with me all the time from 7 o'clock Saturday evening until 6 o'clock Sunday morning [when the police arrested him]. He couldn't have left me."[92]

Smith filled in a few more details for the police, saying they came from Seavanger, Norway, together. Since then, they had been roommates at the Hislop home and the Laguna Street address. Lukherath was a troubled soul and had moved from job to job since they arrived. Finally, a month ago, he got Lukherath a position at the sausage factory.

Everything in the men's stories checked out except the times. They were off by a half hour here and there, but the discrepancies didn't prove Lukherath killed young Hislop.

Circumstantial evidence pointed to Herman Lukherath as the killer of young Robbie Hislop. San Francisco Call. May 27, 1901.

Besides, the only evidence against Herman Lukherath was that he asked Robbie Hislop to bring his mail to his new address. Charles Seibt, who owned a candy store at 1944 Market Street, told detectives Lukherath and the boy had visited his shop the previous week.

Seibt said Lukherath bought Robbie 10 cents worth of candy and promised him 25 cents for every letter he delivered to him.

Another witness placed Lukherath on the scene at the time of the murder. James Duffey told detectives he saw Lukherath loitering near the Hislop home, but Lukherath and Schmidt denied being on Haight Street that night. So, who was telling the truth?

The physical evidence favored Lukherath. His clothes would have been soaked if he had been standing outside the Hislop home in the rain. Yet, when the police arrested Lukherath the following day, the clothes lying on the floor by his bed were "perfectly dry." That seemed to prove he wasn't the man Duffey saw.

Robbie's brother, George Hislop, was another character that bore watching. He arrived at the Hislop home moments after his parents learned that Robbie had been injured.

"Robbie's been hurt," said his mother. "Hurry and get the police."

Instead, George insisted on seeing his brother. Finally, he went to the corner grocery store and asked the owner to call the police.

And then, after summoning the police, George went downtown to meet his girlfriend at the California Theater rather than returning home to check on his brother. Why didn't he show more interest in finding out what was wrong with his brother? It was suspicious.

Even the police had doubts they had the right guy. Still, they wouldn't let him go. "If Lukherath is guilty of this atrocious murder," said Captain Seymour, "he is the cleverest villain I ever met. His cool demeanor and readiness to answer all questions in the face of the serious accusation against him are sufficient to mystify even a Sherlock Holmes. However, I intend to hold him until the mystery is cleared up."[93]

The police released Lukherath a week later, on June 1. Captain Seymour told reporters he was convinced Lukherath wasn't the murderer.

Finally, all the police were left with was the hatchet found near the Hislop home. The red spots on it proved to be blood, but that was no help until they discovered who it belonged to.

Dozens of people came to the station house hoping to identify their lost hatchet. Numerous stories appeared in the papers describing it, begging the owner to claim it. But no one did.

"Who owns it?" demanded the *San Francisco Call*. The hatchet was well used. Its owner should have missed it, yet no one stepped forward to claim it. Why?[94]

And then, on June 5, detectives learned the hatchet found in the vacant lot near the Hislop home was likely not the murder weapon. Instead, George Bonnet's son left it after playing with some neighborhood kids.[95]

And then there's the strange case of Tomaso Lopez. He appeared in Redwood City a few days after Robbie Hislop's murder, saying he'd just walked there from San Francisco. Several people overheard him muttering that he'd been accused of murdering a small boy there. So, detectives thought he might have killed Robbie Hislop, but all hope of proving it disappeared when Lopez hung himself in the county jail. When his pockets were searched, detectives found a crumpled-up page from the *San Francisco Examiner* featuring Hislop's murder.

Lopez's wife soon erased any hopes that he was the killer. Her husband was home with her when Robbie Hislop was murdered. And as for the news story found in his pocket, her husband made a "practice of cutting out newspaper stories of murders when in his cups."[96]

Tomaso Lopez was not the killer.

Three days later, the papers gave up all hope of finding Hislop's killer. "Unless the murderer surrenders himself or some tangible clue is obtained," said the reporter, "the awful murder of the unfortunate boy will forever remain a mystery."[97]

After that, interest in Robbie Hislop's murder quickly faded away. The police had no idea who killed him and put the case on the back burner, pending further clues. And the press locked Robbie Hislop away in their toolbox of unsolved murders. Now and then, when another senseless killing occurred, they'd pull Robbie's murder out as an example of how helpless the police were in solving such crimes.

The Strange Case of Nora Fuller (1902)

Fifteen-year-old Nora Fuller left home at 5:15 p.m. Saturday to meet John Bennett at the Popular Restaurant on Geary Street. Bennett had placed a help-wanted advertisement in the *San Francisco Chronicle* and *San Francisco Examiner*.

"Wanted—young white girl to take care of baby. Good home and good wages."

On January 11, Nora received the following response:

"Miss Fuller: in response to my advertisement, kindly call at the Popular Restaurant, 55 Geary Street, and inquire for Mr. John Bennett at 1 o'clock. If you can't come at 1, come at 6. John Bennett."

Her brother, Louis Parlane, received a phone call from Nora an hour later, saying she got offered a position as a nurse girl at $20 per month. She was at 1500 Geary Street, where Mr. Bennett lived, and he wanted her to start immediately.

Fifteen-year-old Nora Fuller created a media sensation when she disappeared while applying for a job on January 11, 1902. (San Francisco Call. April 9, 1902.)

Alice Fuller, the girl's mother, didn't like that idea. "Tell her to bring home those groceries I gave her the money to buy," said Mrs. Fuller. "Then, she can start work tomorrow."

"All right. Tell momma I'll bring them," said the girl, and the call quickly dropped. That was the last that was heard from her.

When Nora hadn't come home by Sunday, Alice Fuller contacted the police.

At first, she thought her ex-husband James Parlane might have kidnapped the girl. He was reported to have drowned many years ago, but his body never turned up.

Nora was born in China as Eleonora Parlane, where her father worked as the chief engineer of the steamer Tai-Wo, running cargo off the China coast. Reports said Parlane steamed out of Shanghai for Han Kow in July 1890. He fell asleep in a chair on the hurricane deck, and when a deckhand went to get him, he was gone. It was supposed that he'd been swept overboard in the storm.[98]

Detectives quickly discounted that theory as the ravings of a madwoman and turned their attention toward John Bennett.

John Bennett had frequented the Popular Restaurant on and off for fifteen years. The restaurant employees described him as in his mid-forties, about 5 feet 9, heavyset, with a thick mustache, reddish-brown hair, and a slight droop to his right eyelid.

F. W. Krone, the proprietor of the Popular Restaurant, said Bennett "left instructions with me that should a young girl call for him, I should bring her at once to his table. At about 6 o'clock, he left the restaurant. I noticed him walking up and down the sidewalk, but I do not remember having seen him meet anybody."[99] In another interview, Krone said, "I have always regarded him as a faker and have been distrustful of him from the start."[100]

No one can say whether the girl came, just that Nora and John Bennett disappeared at about the same time.

Detective Coleman assumed that Nora, like thousands of other girls in the city, got tired of her circumstances and ran away from home. "I know they are wrong," said Mrs. Fuller. "A mother's instinct is better than their training."[101]

Be that as it may, grocer A. Menke said Nora often used the phone at his store to call someone at a hotel. And just recently, she told him she was going away.

Ray Zertona, a Menke's Grocery Store clerk, said Nora met a man who resembled Bennett outside the store that night. She "seemed glad to meet her friend, and together the couple walked down Central Avenue toward the McAllister Street cars."[102]

When Detective Coleman went to Bennett's address at 1500 Geary Street, he discovered an empty lot.

Hugh Grant, Alice Fuller's attorney, became a primary suspect in the investigation. Because Nora frequently visited his office carrying messages from her mother, he became a person of interest. Then, in September, Grant bought Nora a dress for $22.50, which fueled more than a dozen newspaper articles wondering why. What made him buy her an expensive dress?[103]

Alice Fuller described Grant as a "habitual drunk" and womanizer. "Flashily dressed" women frequented his office.[104] Grant's landlady, Mrs. A. M. Brown, agreed that he was a drunken eccentric, yet he spent much time at the Fuller house, often taking dinner there. However, the story behind his frequent visits was never fully explained. Was Grant having an affair with Alice Fuller? Was he after Nora? Or was there something else going on?

The manager of the Francisco Hotel complained that Grant hadn't paid his bill, then threw in that he was at times effeminate and wasn't happy until he received a lace bedspread.

Whatever connection Grant had to the girl, he didn't kill Nora Fuller. Grant didn't match the description of the man who waited to meet Nora at the Popular Restaurant. And he didn't rent the home at Sutter Street or purchase the furniture or bedding found there.

Madge Graham, a close friend of Nora Fuller, said she overheard Nora telephoning Bennett several times in December. "She would laugh and tell me to go away and not listen to her when she called him up. She never told me anything about him except that he was a friend."

Madge painted an entirely different picture of Nora than her mother gave.

"She often deceived her mother. I know that. She knew lots of people her mother didn't know about and had money that she used to hide in her stocking. She knew a good many boys and offered to introduce me to one."[105]

After finding Nora's body, the police asked Madge why she had never said anything about Nora's relationship with Bennett.

"Because I didn't think it was necessary," said Madge. "Nobody asked me outright about Bennett, and I didn't think it was necessary to tell."[106]

Any other questions detectives put to her got answered with: "I don't know." "I forget." "I can't remember."

Nora's nude body turned up in a house at 2211 Sutter Street on February 8, 1902, twenty-seven days after she disappeared.

Richard Burns of Umbsen and Co. sent Harry E. Deane to check on the house on February 8 after C. B. Hawkins's lease expired.

He arrived at the house at about 3 p.m. When no one answered the door, he unlocked it and went inside. He found the lower part of the house empty, except for a few circulars and letters scattered along the floor.

"Then I went to the rear room [upstairs]," said Deane, "and when I opened the door, the first thing I saw was some clothes on a chair, apparently some woman's clothes—I got the bright color. So, I stopped and hesitated a moment. Then I started into the room and glanced around quickly." I "saw the bed at the left of the door, and somebody apparently in bed with the covers drawn over."

Deane walked out the door and knocked. When he didn't get an answer, he called out, "Who is there?"

Unsure of what to do, Deane left the house and walked to the corner, where he found Officer James Gill.

Madge Graham, a close confidant of Nora Fuller, who police suspected knew more about the girl's disappearance than she let on. (San Francisco Examiner. March 22, 1902.)

They went back to the house together and found the body. Gill said there was a powerful smell in the room after he lifted the covers. He did not stay in the room very long. Gill walked down to the O'Farrell Street Police Station and notified the Sargent. He dispatched the coroner and Detective Thomas Dillon.[107]

"There were no marks on the body to indicate violence had been used," said Detective Dillon, "and we did not think so until after leaving Umbsen's office and learning that the house had been rented by a man." Nothing looked out of place. The clothing looked like it had been laid out by someone going to bed.[108]

Chief Deputy Coroner Peter J. McCormick later testified that the order of clothing was wrong. The underclothes were on the bottom instead of the top "as they would have been in natural sequence if the person undressing had placed the clothes directly on the chair."[109]

Detective Dillon determined it was either a suicide or natural death and made no further investigation. *The San Francisco Examiner* chuckled. "Evidently, Detective Dillon does not move in the detective fashion of the fiction heroes of Poe, Gaboriau, or Dr. Conan Doyle."[110]

The house was rented on January 8 to C. B. Hawkins, who said he lived at the Golden West Hotel. He bought a mattress, two blankets, a comforter, and two pillows from the Cavanagh Furniture Store on January 9, then ran the ad that lured Nora on January 10. That same day, he bought a bedstead, wire mattress, and chair at the Standard Furniture Company.

The delivery man, P. J. Tobin, said a well-dressed man answered the door when he delivered the furniture. He carried it in and set it up in the upstairs bedroom. Nora Fuller's body was discovered three weeks later in the same bedroom.

On Saturday, January 11, Nora Fuller left her home to meet John Bennett at the Popular Restaurant.

Alice Fuller didn't believe any of it. She said her daughter wouldn't go into a vacant house with a stranger. "She was too timid. She would have stopped at the door, and no inducement could have made her go up that dark stairway. She was too timid and would have scented danger at once."

Mrs. Fuller said the only way someone would have gotten Nora into that house was by drugging her and carrying her up the stairs. "I think it will be found to be true," said Mrs. Fuller, that "she was killed somewhere else, and her body carried there in the darkness of night, in a sack maybe."[111]

It quickly came out that the police mismanaged the crime scene. Detective Dillon determined it was a suicide or natural death, so he didn't catalog the evidence or note where items were found. He also didn't check to see if a struggle had taken place.[112]

The San Francisco Examiner gave up hope after the coroner's inquest. "Who killed Nora Fuller?" they asked. "The coroner's jury could not say. Perhaps, no one but the slayer knows or will ever know."[113]

Toxicologist Dr. Charles L. Morgan placed the time of death as seven to ten days before the body was found. Maybe as far back as twenty to thirty-five days, but he couldn't say with any certainty.[114]

He did find some traces of an apple in the girl's stomach. Alice Fuller said her daughter ate an apple a few hours before she left home that day. That led the coroner's jury to believe Nora died on the night she disappeared.

Autopsy Surgeon Bacigalupi agreed. The girl had been dead for at least seven days. Beyond that, he could not say. There was evidence of an outrage performed on the girl (meaning someone had raped her).[115]

On March 1, detectives apprehended C. A. Seifert in Esparto, California. Seifert was 38 years old, stood five feet eight, and was a licensed pharmacist. He was acquainted with Emma Searight, a friend of Nora Fuller.

Detectives arrested Seifert for taking money under false pretenses, but they suspected he knew more than he let on about the murder of Nora Fuller.

Detectives arrested C. A. Seifert for taking money under false pretenses, but they suspected he knew more than he let on about the murder of Nora Fuller. (San Francisco Call. March 1, 1902.)

Although his attorney warned him not to say anything, Seifert "leaked information" concerning his whereabouts when the girl disappeared and when her body was found.

He was in the Palm Concert Hall on Ellis Street when detectives found Nora Fuller's body, then went to the Turkish Baths on Post Street. When they learned about the discovery of Nora's body, all the men in his party went down to the morgue to view the remains. That was the only time he ever saw Nora Fuller. That should have been a red flag, but detectives let it go.

Seifert hired Emma Searight to promote some perfume. He paid her with tickets to the Juvenile Fairyland Carnival, then asked for them back. She refused. He thought that might be why she mixed him up in the Fuller girl's murder.

When asked why he tried to elude the police, Seifert said he didn't. "If the detectives were scouring the city for me, as they claim, they must have done a very bungling job because I could have been located in an hour by anybody who was not a sleuth."[116]

After Seifert's arrest, the newspapers took their frustrations out on the police.

"The colossal stupidity displayed by captain of detectives Seymour in his management of the Nora

Fuller case reached its climax yesterday when it was demonstrated beyond question that C. A. Seifert, who was arrested at Esparto Friday, ostensibly for embezzlement but actually for complicity in that crime, had no connection with the shocking event."[117]

On March 15, Samuel Raguet, a waiter at the Orpheum Cafe on O'Farrell Street, threw detectives another curveball. He said Madge Graham and Nora Fuller had dinner at the restaurant on January 11 when Nora Fuller disappeared.

Nora Fuller and Chief Seymour. The San Francisco Call blasted Chief Seymour for his "colossal stupidity" and "mismanagement" of the Nora Fuller case. (San Francisco Call. March 10, 1902.)

They arrived at the restaurant at about 6:30 and laughed and giggled for a few minutes. Then, at about 6:40, Madge's guardian, Edward Stearns, and a man who looked like Hugh Grant joined them in a private box.

Madge whispered to the waiter: "That other girl is to be married to that other fellow."[118]

The waiter said Madge was in a good mood laughing and joking all the time, but the other girl "looked to me to be at the point of bursting into tears." The larger man said he had been drinking for two nights and was sick and tired.[119]

Stearns and Grant denied that any such meeting took place.

Unbeknownst to her mother, Nora Fuller tried to secure a position as a showgirl in early December. She applied to an advertisement from the Pacific Coast Theatrical Exchange that offered $20 per week to girls who could sing.[120]

And then, there were the drunken loonies like E. J. Dempsey. In early March, he stopped two policemen at Seventh Street and Broadway and told them, "There is no doubt about me being the man. I slew Nora Fuller."

On investigation, it proved the "liquor he had drunk had got the better of his imagination."[121]

In April, detectives located Nora's best friend, Estelle Baker (a vaudeville performer), in Williams, Arizona. She said Nora and Bennett had seen each other for at least four months before her disappearance. Nora had visited the Olympic and several different resorts with him.

In mid-March, Maud Graham made a startling announcement. "I believe that my daughter Madge knows who killed Nora Fuller. My girl and the dead girl were the closest kinds of chums. I know they exchanged secrets.

"As sure as I am alive," said Mrs. Graham, "I believe Madge is afraid to tell what she knows. I think the man who killed Nora has seen Madge and told her he would serve her as he did Nora if she told on him."[122]

Then she suggested the reason Madge wouldn't say anything might be that she would implicate herself. First, the girls had planned to run away just before Christmas, but then Nora backed out because she didn't want to leave her mother.

She hinted that Madge and Nora had spent more than a little time on the wild side. She had a memorandum that showed "the two girls were rather well acquainted with things they ought not to have known."[123]

In his book *Celebrated Criminal Cases of America*, Thomas B. Duke blamed Charles B. Hadley, an accountant and subscription collector, with *The San Francisco Examiner*.[124]

Carrie Dixon, his common-law wife, confirmed that he did not sleep at his home on January 11, the night Nora Fuller disappeared.[125]

It later turned out that Hadley had embezzled money from the paper, then disappeared. Hadley left so abruptly he didn't bother to withdraw the $1500 he had in the bank.

"I am sure that something terrible has caused Hadley to drop from sight," Carrie Dixon told investigators. "He has been acting like a crazy man for the past week. I noticed that his hair was turning white."[126]

His appearance was much like that of the mysterious John Bennett, except he was clean-shaven. The girl he lived with filled in the blanks. She said Hadley often wore a fake mustache purchased at a Japanese store on Larkin Street.[127]

Detectives had an artist add a mustache to Hadley's picture and showed it to people who had identified Bennett. All but one person said Hadley and Bennett were one and the same.

Both men also enjoyed porterhouse steaks, particularly the tenderloin.

C. B. Hadley disappeared from his job as an accountant at the San Francisco Examiner on the same day Nora Fuller went missing. That led detectives to think he might have been involved in her murder. (San Francisco Call. May 2, 1907.)

By the time detectives learned about Hadley, he had already skipped town.

Investigators believe Hadley, who was then going by J. H. Hanley, "blew his brains out" in Golden Gate Park in early July 1904. Deputy Coroner Charles Meehan said the "resemblance is very close." *Moreover, the San Francisco Chronicle* reported, "his verification of this description tallies in every detail with that of Hadley."[128]

As far as the police are concerned, the 1902 strangling death of Nora Fuller is an unsolved homicide.

The Russian Hill Murder
(1904)

Leon Soeder joined a conspiracy to murder his brother-in-law, Joseph Blaise, to collect the fat insurance policy he planned to put on his life. At first, the police believed two or three more men were involved in the plot.

"Give us enough time," said Detective Tom Gibson. "We will make this the most interesting murder trial that has ever occurred in San Francisco."[129]

Soeder traveled to Hun, Alsace Lorraine, to lure his brother-in-law with the promise of the easy money waiting for him in America. It sounded like the answer to his prayers for the impoverished German living in a filthy hovel with his wife and five kids, especially since Soeder offered to pay all the expenses for his new start.

After arriving in New York, Soeder applied for two $10,000 insurance policies on Blaise's life. When the insurance companies turned him down because Blaise was just a hotel keeper and cook, Soeder switched gears.

The two men traveled to San Francisco, where Soeder applied for a $10,000 policy with the Pacific Mutual Company. They turned it down flat and issued a $3,000 policy with Blaises's wife listed as the beneficiary.

A week later, the two men returned to the Pacific Mutual Company and took out two $3,000 life insurance policies. Blaise listed Soeder as the beneficiary on his policy, and Soeder listed Blaise as the beneficiary. They paid the $103 premium and left.

Ten days later, Blaise died at the foot of Russian Hill.

William Horan discovered the body on Taylor Street between Green and Vallejo at 8 a.m. on Monday, January 10, 1904. The murderer stabbed Blaise in the throat, then plunged the knife into his head, tearing a huge gash across the scalp. Officer Russell, the police sketch artist, determined the murderer selected the darkest spot at the foot of Russian Hill. The man could not have fallen to his death as was first suspected because the body didn't have any bruises or fractured bones.[130]

Sergeant Christianson, the first policeman on the scene, said nothing indicated a struggle had occurred.[131]

Detectives discovered a letter in the dead man's pocket that identified him, where he lived, and mentioned Leon Soeder's name.

An artist's sketch of some of the people involved in the Leon Soeder trial. (The San Francisco Call. January 27, 1904)

Police quickly tracked Soeder down to 827 Jackson Street and questioned him.

Soeder said they ate at the Original Mexican Restaurant on Broadway Street at about 5 p.m., then returned home. Blaise took a walk around 6 p.m., and he hadn't heard from him since then.

Soeder told detectives Blaise came to the United States with $200, mostly gold coins. He had $90 on his person when he went for a walk. They spent the rest of the money on the insurance policy in favor of Blaise's wife. Soeder didn't bother mentioning the other two policies he took on Blaise's life.

His story seemed straightforward and truthful, so the police released him.

Later that day, a reporter for *The San Francisco Call* questioned S. M. Marks of the Pacific Mutual Company about the policies. Marks told him Soeder tried to purchase a $10,000 policy, but they would only write one for $3,000. He also mentioned the other two policies.

The reporter shared that information with the police, and Soeder was taken into custody again.

His landlady, Mrs. Joseph Nieblas, said she heard the men leave at 5 p.m. but did not hear them return at 6 p.m., as Soeder claimed. Later, she recanted her testimony at the preliminary hearing and said she went to bed at 10:15 p.m. She would not have known if Soeder had come in after that.[132]

Several suspicious things turned up as the police began to investigate Soeder.

Police found a knife in his house that they believed was the murder weapon. The day after Blaise died, Soeder took his suit to the cleaners. He told police he didn't own a gun. And then later, he admitted he pawned a .38 caliber Smith & Wesson hammerless revolver at Levi's Pawn Shop on Stockton Street in the name of Sam Norman.[133]

Detective Gibson discovered Soeder did not return to his room on the night of the murder. Instead, he came back the following day to get the insurance policies from Blaise's briefcase. As a result, he had the policies in his pocket when the police arrested him.

Ten days after Blaise's Murder, Detective Thomas Gibson said he "had enough evidence against Soeder to hang him."

Soeder's alibi didn't mean anything, Gibson had busted it wide-open, or so he thought.

Soeder spent the night before the murder at the O. K. Saloon with his buddy Frank Cannon. Cannon saw the two men having dinner at the Original Mexican restaurant at 721 Broadway Street. But unfortunately, he couldn't tell the police the direction the men set off in when they left the restaurant.

"After he killed his brother-in-law Soeder went to his room on Jackson Street," said Gibson. He "changed the gray suit he wore for the black one in which he appeared when he went down to the O. K. Saloon on Pacific Street.

"He did not go right into the dancehall but stood under the archway and nodded to Theresa King and another woman in the place. His object was to furnish himself with an alibi.

"He went out and then returned to the saloon and talked with one of the girls. His attempt to form an alibi was cunningly planned, but we have enough evidence to break it down."[134]

This wasn't the first run-in Soeder had with the police. He'd been arrested in 1894 for robbing A. Johnson's restaurant at 28 Montgomery Street. Soeder spent three years in San Quentin for that.

Soeder became involved in a counterfeiting scheme in 1900. When things didn't go as he expected, Soeder turned his partner, Goadello, in for a $50 reward.

When detectives searched Soeder's rooms at the Five-Mile House, they found two bottles of hydrocyanic acid in his trunk.

Katherine Flatley, Soeder's fiancée, pounded another nail into his coffin when she told police he expected to receive $7,000 from Germany shortly. Soeder left the trunk in her home while he traveled to Germany. She saw several small bottles in a valise at that time.

Katharine Flatley was a real piece of work.

Leon Soeder, with a big question mark. Did he do it? (The San Francisco Call. January 17, 1904)

She had been keeping company with Soeder for six months but never intended to marry him because she "never liked his looks."[135] When he left for Germany, Soeder asked her to return the jewelry he had given her. She refused. When he returned from Germany, he asked her to return the jewelry. When she said no, he sought a warrant for her arrest from Marin County.

Ten days before Blaise's death, someone broke into Miss Flatley's home and stole several bottles from Soeder's valise. The burglar poisoned her dog during the robbery.

The Friday before the murder, Soeder reclaimed the trunk and replaced the two bottles of hydrocyanic acid. Detectives are sure Soeder broke into Flatley's home.

The police theorized that Soeder initially planned to poison Blaise, then switched gears at the last minute.

It wasn't the first time Soeder had attempted insurance fraud. His wife, a Mexican girl, died mysteriously at Petaluma in 1903, and he collected a $2,000 policy on her life.

His previous wife, Elizabeth Nefs, left him and returned to Germany in September 1888. Soeder thought she died shortly after that, but he wasn't sure. Soon after his wife's death, Soeder's ranch house burned.

He tried to collect insurance, but the insurance company refused to pay.[136]

The coroner's inquest began on January 27.

Detective Gibson complained that he needed more time to gather evidence, but Coroner Leland overrode him. He said it was an "unwritten rule" that the inquest should be conducted before the preliminary hearing.[137]

William Hogan, the millhand who found the body, told the coroner's jury he thought the man was drunk, so he kicked him. When Blaise didn't move, he rushed off to notify Officer Christianson, who lived nearby.

"There was a pool of blood on the ground beneath the neck," said Detective Armstrong, "which had a gaping wound in it." He searched for a weapon but didn't find anything.

"There was no evidence of a struggle, no cuts on the hands, only the wound on the neck and a laceration of the scalp." The trousers were stiff, leading him to believe the body had laid there for some time.[138]

Maria Vallarta, the owner of the Original Mexican Restaurant, changed her story and said the two men left between 6 and 6:15, not 7:30, as she had previously told Detective Gibson. Though not a significant difference, it moved the time of death closer to 8 p.m.

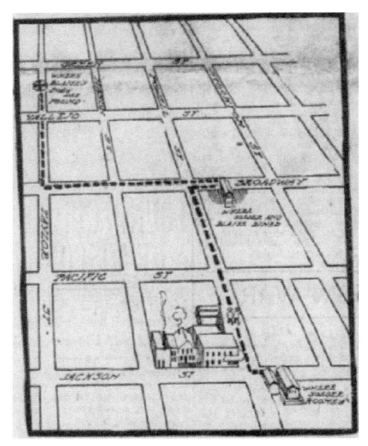

Sketch map showing the location of Joseph Blaise's murder in relation to their rooms and the Original Mexican Restaurant, where Blaise was last seen alive. (The San Francisco Call. January 14, 1904)

Several agents from the Pacific Mutual Insurance Company testified about Soeder's application. J. W. Fowler said Soeder wanted a $10,000 policy, but the company would not issue a policy that big for a cook. Eventually, they issued a $3,000 policy for which the premium was $102.60. Soeder gave him a $50 deposit on the fee.

City Chemist A. C. Bothe testified that he didn't find any poisons in Blaise's system. Based on the digestion of the food found in the stomach, he set the time of death as no later than an hour and a half to two hours after the men finished eating. That would put the time of death between 8:30 and 9.[139]

Professor Thomas Price found traces of blood on the dagger in Leon Soeder's room. There was blood where the blade joined the handle and where the handle held the blade. What he didn't know was if it was human blood.[140]

After hearing all the evidence, the coroner's jury ruled that Joseph Blaise came to a violent death at the hands of a party or parties unknown.[141]

No one doubted that Soeder was a bad character. The problem was the police had the motive (money) and Soeder's previous arrest record, but they didn't have the necessary evidence to tie Soeder to the crime.

In mid-February, detectives learned Soeder's father had died under suspicious circumstances in Germany several years before. Couple that with the disappearance of Soeder's first wife and the mysterious death of his second wife, and it confirmed he bore more watching.

The information from Germany also said Blaise only had $17 when he left home, not the $200 Soeder claimed he did. That tended to rule robbery out as the motive for his murder. The police also discovered several letters Blaise wrote to his wife in Germany. It came out that Blaise did not want to come to America. He only did so because he was desperate for a job. Blaise lived in a filthy shack in Alsace-Lorraine with five other family members.[142]

Soeder's trial began in May 1904.

Dr. William G. Mizner, the medical examiner for the Pacific Mutual Insurance Company, lightened things up for a moment.

When Soeder got mad because the company wouldn't write the $10,000 policy, the doctor said, "I suppose the company is afraid you will do up Blaise. You don't intend to kill him, do you?"

Soeder was unsure how to react or what to say. Finally, he smiled and said, "I'm not going to harm him."

Soeder's defense attorney, General Edward Salomon, contended that his client was "as innocent of the crime as a newborn babe and that the murder was done by others for the purpose of robbery."[143]

John Cooper, Soeder's cellmate, took the stand on May 18. He testified that Soeder confessed to the crime, saying he killed his brother-in-law.

Strangely, the judge warned him that if he was lying, the penalty for sending an innocent man to his death was execution.

Cooper thought about it for several minutes. He glanced around the courtroom nervously, then said he did not wish to change his testimony.

Soeder did it.[144]

He told him the story in bits and pieces over two weeks. First, Soeder said he hit Blaise over the head with a broken shovel. "Then he stood over him with his left knee pressed to Blaise's back and slit his brother-in-law's throat with a knife held in his right hand."[145]

"A man without money was no good in this country," said Soeder. "He would as soon murder his brother-in-law as a stranger."

The prosecution produced a map Soeder supposedly drew on the edge of a newspaper to help Cooper understand the landscape where the murder occurred.

Soeder's attorney put him on the witness stand in a last-ditch effort to save his neck, but it didn't help. The jury found Soeder guilty of murder on May 23, 1904.

Judge Cook sentenced him to death.

Deputy Sheriff Edward J. Kerwin escorted Soeder to San Quentin on September 15, where he was to await his execution.[146]

Two years later, in October 1906, the California Supreme Court sustained the ruling of the Superior Court. As a result, Leon Soeder was to die by hanging.[147]

Before his hanging, Soeder donated his body to Dr. C. F. Millar at Central Emergency Hospital for dissection. "He did not want the soul of his victim to haunt his remains."[148]

Soeder spoke to the press before going to the gallows. "I am the victim of perjury. I never made any confession. That was a manufactured confession. Detective Tom Gibson manufactured that confession."[149]

Leon Soeder was hanged on March 29, 1907. He feigned toughness throughout the ordeal, but on the gallows, he staggered and fainted as the executioner arranged the noose around his neck.

Some California Women Who Got Away With Murder (1911-1914)

California prosecutors found themselves in a quandary at the turn of the century. Male jurors were reluctant to convict women

"If women can commit murders and juries will not convict them, what is to be done?" asked District Attorney W. H. L. Hynes.[150]

Hynes explained that it was almost impossible to convict a woman of murder. "Even where the act is admitted, premeditated, and motives are apparent.

"The woman will testify that she has suffered abuse from or has violated the conventional moral code with the deceased.

"Even where a man may have no hope of escaping the penalty of his act, a woman may feel reasonably sure of immunity."[151]

Former District Attorney Fickert took it a step further, "saying a woman uses her sex as a shield. And if the accused woman is pretty or has a glamor of romance about her, it is next to impossible to convict her."[152]

It wasn't just a California problem, though. Women everywhere were getting away with murder because male jurors couldn't find it in their hearts to convict them.

San Francisco experienced five such cases between 1911 and 1914 alone. Chicago had dozens of women killers who walked away, acquitted of their crimes. The few women that were convicted were minorities or less than pretty.

In San Francisco, Leah Alexander admitted to murdering her married lover, Joseph Van Baalen, yet the jury found her not guilty.

"Anna T. Langley was treated as a guest of honor at the city jail" after she was arrested for murdering her husband, reported the *San Francisco Examiner*.[153]

Grace Shields stabbed Melvin La Selve in the heart during a lover's spat on July 24, 1912. The jury deliberated for three hours before acquitting her. Finally, they determined it was self-defense.

Mary Sudall shot her husband, Joseph Sudall, after he asked her to return her wedding ring. After listening to Mary's story about how he frequently abused her, the jury acquitted her, saying it was self-defense.

Millie Drown shot her husband, Archer Drown, while he slept. Then, she phoned his girlfriend to arrange a luncheon appointment at the woman's home. The jury deliberated for less than thirty minutes before it acquitted her. She was found not guilty because of temporary insanity.

It was hard to explain, but male jurors refused to see women as killers, even when they confessed or there was an abundance of witnesses to the crime.

Leah Alexander

Leah Alexander had been going with Joseph Van Baalen for over a year, but they only became intimate after he gave her an engagement ring and promised to marry her.

"He gave me the wedding ring when we boarded the Overland for New York," said Leah. They bought their tickets and signed in at the hotel as Mr. & Mrs. Van Baalen.

Not long after that, they went to Cuba. That's when she learned he was married. "I left him after that and returned to my home in Los Angeles," said Leah. But, of course, she couldn't stay away.

Leah went to Van Baalen's apartment twice, trying to win him back. The first time, Mrs. Van Baalen slapped her face and ordered her to leave. The next time, Leah argued with Joseph Van Baalen for fifteen minutes. Finally, Van Baalen told her to get lost. He was through with her.

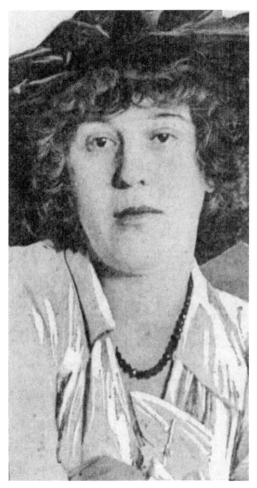

Leah Alexander was one of four women in San Francisco who got away with murder between 1911 and 1914. (San Francisco Chronicle. January 28, 1914.)

Not long after that, on Saturday, August 18, 1913, Leah Alexander burst into Joseph D. Van Baalen's office at the *San Francisco Chronicle* and fired five bullets.

Three shots hit the target. One pierced Van Baalen's left shoulder, the second his left thigh, and the third tore through his back and intestines, emerging through his abdomen.

Later, at the police station, Leah told detectives she'd known Van Baalen for three years. They fell in love. He promised to marry her after his divorce came through, and then he dumped her.

She caught him "avoiding her, refusing to meet her, ignoring her, and refusing to speak to her over the phone." However, the last straw was when she caught him paying attention to another woman.[154]

The Tuesday before the shooting, Van Baalen refused to take Leah to the theater. Instead, he walked his new assistant, Rhoda Thompson, to her home.

Leah lost hope after that and tried to kill herself. Dr. B. D. Plymer testified that she had "taken 45 grains of verinol, one-sixth of a grain of strychnine and had lain unconscious for twenty hours or so." Plymer visited Leah on Thursday and Friday to ensure she was okay.[155]

"Finally, I made up my mind," said Leah. She walked down to Market Street, bought a gun and a box of cartridges, loaded it, and went to Van Baalen's office.[156]

"I went into his room and found it full of people, so I asked him if I could see him a moment. He took me into an inside room."

"I do not believe you're in love with me," he said with a sneer.

"Well, aren't you in love with me?"

"I was once," he said, "but that's all over now. I don't have to explain to you, and I won't. You get out. I'm through with you."

Leah was crazy with anger but calmly asked him for a drink. He left the room to get her a glass of water. When Van Baalen returned, Leah "pointed the pistol at him and began firing blindly."

Van Baalen ran out of the office and down the corridor. All the while, she kept pulling the trigger.

He fell in front of the elevator. Leah bent down over him and fired again. All she remembered after that was telling someone, "Don't tell my mother. It would kill her."[157]

The police dragged Leah to the hospital and showed her to Van Baalen before the doctors operated on him.

"Don't lock her up," he said. "It's all right. Don't lock her up. Don't be unkind to her."

When asked why she shot him, Van Baalen answered, "because she was crazy." Then he passed into unconsciousness.

A few hours later, he was dead. Joseph Van Baalen died at the Central Emergency Hospital at 1:38 a.m. on Sunday, August 19.

Leah Alexander was acquitted on January 31, 1914. Even though several doctors testified that Leah was sane, the jury decided she was "temporarily insane" when she shot Van Baalen.

When asked what she planned to do after hearing the verdict, Leah said, "sleep." And then explained that she didn't want to kill Van Baalen, "but God knows, he deserved it."[158]

The following day, she had more time to think about what came next. Several theater companies had offered her roles in their new productions, hoping to capitalize on her fame, but she turned them down.

"I want to get away from here," she said. "I want the world to forget what I have done and been." The thing she dreaded the most was hearing people say, "Leah Alexander. Oh, the girl that—."

She was ready for a new start.[159]

Anna Langley

Anna Langley married the wrong man. She met James Langley when she was fourteen; he was twenty-two. At the time, James was well-dressed and handsome. He talked about the great life they'd have together. However, her parents warned her to stay away from him, saying he was trouble.

She was young and foolish and believed him. They ran away and eloped the following year when she turned fifteen. The troubles started almost immediately.

James started calling her names and beating her for no reason. Then, he lost his job. So, she went to work as a stenographer and supported him while he drank and gambled her meager salary away.

If she had to guess, Anna figured her husband worked eight weeks out of the eighteen months they were married. He always told her he had nice hands, too nice to spoil with work. The last straw was when he stole their marriage documents and the $90 she'd saved for a house.

The Tuesday before she shot him, Jim twisted her arm, forcing her to scream. Then, he threw one of the neighbor ladies out of her room, packed his stuff, and left.

The following day, she trailed him to the Bare & Phillips Saloon at 2115 Mission Street. She coaxed him out, and they went to a nearby restaurant. She wanted to talk, but he abused her and called her vile names.

They left the restaurant and wound up back near the saloon. Anna walked down the street, traded her gold watch for a revolver at a Market Street pawnshop, then returned to the saloon.

When she got there, Jim held up her bank book and asked for $20. He insisted they go to the bank and get the money, calling her an "evil bitch" when she refused.

"Come home," she said.

He called her an "evil bitch" again and started back into the saloon. Anna hesitated momentarily. One report says he pushed her into the gutter. Anna pulled the revolver out of the folds of her dress and opened fire.[160]

"It was the first time the girl held a loaded revolver," said the *San Francisco Examiner*, sounding almost proud of her. "Of the four shots, she fired, only one found its mark." But it did the trick, going straight through James Langley's heart.

Anna told her story to the press a few days after the shooting.

"Anna T. Langley was treated as a guest of honor at the city jail" after she was arrested for murdering her husband, reported the San Francisco Examiner.

"I shot him because he told me he had no more respect for me than a woman of the Barbary Coast.

"As soon as we were married, he began to strike and insult me. He spent every dollar he could get for drink."

She stayed with him because she loved him and thought he would change. James said he had small hands and didn't want to spoil them by working.

"He locked me out at night," continued Anna. "I used to walk the streets until I was cold and tired from looking for him."[161]

Anna testified before the grand jury on August 4. "It was one of dreariest stories that this or any other grand jury ever heard," said the *San Francisco Examiner*. It "was filled with mean and soul-dragging details," explaining why she had to kill her husband.[162]

Whatever she said, her words must have been convincing. The grand jury ruled that "James Langley came to his death from a gunshot wound. The shot being fired by Anna Langley, his wife, while she was temporarily insane as a result of the continuous intoxication and abuse on the part of her husband."[163]

The *San Francisco Chronicle* portrayed Anna as a hero in the next day's edition.

"Remarkable scenes were witnessed at the San Francisco Jail yesterday evening," said the paper, "when jurymen, lawyers, and reporters united in cheering Miss Anna Langley, a beautiful girl of 19, who shot and killed her husband a few days ago."

Anna was taken back to jail after testifying before the grand jury. A few minutes later, the jurors visited the jail. They told Anna she was to be released on her own recognizance.

Some of the jurors bought her flowers. Others gave her money to help cover her bills. And "then someone called for 'three cheers' for this plucky little woman."[164] Soon, passersby outside the jail took up the cheering.

On December 1, District Attorney James F. Brennan asked the court to drop the charges against Anna Langley after the grand jury refused to return an indictment against her.[165] He agreed that the shooting was justified.

Grace Shields

Grace Shields killed Melvin La Selve during a lover's spat on July 24, 1912. Unfortunately, her case didn't garner the headlines some of the other female killings did because Grace and her victim were colored.

La Selve owned the Bancroft Bar, a negro resort, at 234 Townsend Street. Grace Shields had a room above the bar. They'd been together for about four years, and La Selve had abused her for most of that time.

They started arguing at 6 p.m. La Selve pulled out a pocketknife and slashed her. The blade slit her leg open so severely that doctors believed it would need to be amputated. Still, she fought him off. Finally, Grace wrestled the weapon away from him and plunged it deep into La Selve's chest. He fell to the floor with the blade stuck in his heart.[166]

Grace Shields was tried before Judge Lawlor in February 1913. The jury deliberated for three hours before acquitting her. They determined that Grace killed Melvin La Selve in self-defense.[167]

Mary Sudall

If any woman profiled in this article deserved to do time, it'd be Mary Sudall. She had a history of committing violent acts against her husband.

The couple had experienced a bumpy, violence-filled relationship. At the divorce hearing, it came out Mary had jammed a pair of shears in her husband's left eye, partially blinding him. And then, a month before she shot her ex-husband, a neighbor saw Mary chasing him down the street with a revolver in her hand.

Joseph Sudall went to his former wife's home at 442A Twenty-fifth Avenue to retrieve her wedding ring. It was a family heirloom that had belonged to his mom and grandmother. He gave it to his wife when they married, and now he wanted it back.

Mary told the police her ex-husband came to her house at about 3:45 p.m. He forced his way in when she opened the door. Then he started arguing about the rent.

She ran inside to call the O'Farrell Street Police Station. A policeman came, but when he learned James Sudall owned part of the house, he said he couldn't do anything and left.

"Then Joe resumed his argument," said Mary. He was very angry. When she refused to give him the ring, Joe "seized a claw-hammer and a pair of shears and attacked me. I ran outside and then back in again toward the vestibule with Sudall chasing me."[168]

She fired three shots, hitting him twice. Joseph staggered down a flight of steps, went into the yard, leaned against a fence, then fell to the ground.

He was taken to the Central Hospital, where he died a few days later.

Mary admitted having a revolver but said she did not fire it. And then she stopped, refusing to say more.

Mary didn't have anything good to say about her husband at her trial in early December.

"He often beat me and threatened my life," she said. "On that day, he came into the house and swore he was going to kill me with a hammer, and I shot. That is all I remember."[169]

The jury deliberated for a half hour before acquitting Mary Sudall.

Millie Drown

Millie Drown shot her husband, Archer Drown, while he slept in their Lakeside District home in Oakland. Then, she phoned his girlfriend, May Millar, to arrange a luncheon appointment at the woman's home. When she arrived, Millie said her husband was delayed but would be along shortly.

A few minutes later, as Millar was preparing the salad, Millie pulled a gun from her stocking and placed the barrel against the woman's head. She pulled the trigger three times. Fortunately, the weapon jammed and wouldn't fire.[170]

After that, she ran out of the house and drove across the bay to San Francisco, where she attended the Portola Festival with friends. Midway through her visit, Millie began to cry, saying her husband was dead, but she never explained what had happened.

One of the women she was with drove her back to Oakland, where they found Arthur Drown dead in his bed. There were two bullet holes in his chest.

A note on the chiffonier said, "Precious Mother in heaven— forgive me for killing myself. I simply can't help it. I am going to lose Archer. He is in love with another woman. Forgive me."[171]

When the police questioned her, Millie admitted to shooting her husband. She told detectives her husband arrived home after midnight, saying he'd been at a smoker. "I made a sarcastic remark, and we quarreled. He slapped my face. I could not sleep. I thought about him and this other woman until I could stand it no longer.

"I decided to kill myself and took the revolver from under his pillow and took a shot, but my hand slipped, and the bullet passed through my nightdress."

Her husband woke up for a few minutes, then went back to sleep, unconcerned. That's when she shot him.

Mrs. Millar told police it was all a story. Millie most likely shot her husband in his sleep without warning. "I

warned him that his wife had threatened to shoot him,"
said Millar. "He was on his guard."[172]

*Millie Drown shot her husband in his sleep because she feared he would leave
her for his girlfriend. A jury acquitted her, saying she was temporarily insane.
(San Francisco Examiner. October 26, 1913.)*

The *San Francisco Chronicle* covered the trial as if it was a
fashion show, reporting that Millie "was faultlessly

gowned in black and wore a stunning hat of the same color." And like a trooper, "she showed no emotion whatever" as the prosecutor read the charges against her.[173]

Prosecutor H. L. Hynes's closing statement demanded the jury think carefully before deciding Millie Drown's fate.

"What woman can you recall who has been convicted of murder? I tell you, gentlemen, the condition is becoming alarming. It has got to the point where women have no regard for the law. It is reaching a position where women can kill with impunity.

"Even the lobbies applaud now when testimony is given against the prosecution. I say we are coming to the place where women can take the life of a man and get nothing less than manslaughter if she gets that. I am not asking you to hang this woman, but she committed cold-blooded, willful, deliberate murder.

"Women have no right to go out and commit murder any more than a man has. If they are mistreated by their husbands, they should go to the divorce court. This kind of thing must stop."[174]

The jury deliberated for less than a half hour before it acquitted Millie Drown. She was found not guilty because of temporary insanity.

The prosecution motioned to have Millie locked away in an asylum, but the defense attorneys objected, saying she was temporarily insane when she shot her husband, not now. So, Judge Ogden finally gave up and let Millie Drown walk away a free woman.

District Attorney Hynes just shook his head. He suggested setting Millie free encouraged women whose husbands had life insurance and a good income to go out and kill them. Afterward, they could walk away scot-free with the insurance money and income. In Millie Drown's case, she collected $12,000 in life insurance and a $100 a month income (roughly $2800 today).[175]

The Movie Star and the Starlet (1921)

Roscoe Conkling Arbuckle, stage name "Fatty" Arbuckle, was one of the hottest stars of the silent film era. The thirty-four-year-old stood five feet eight and tipped the scales at 268, hence the nickname "Fatty." The name dogged Arbuckle throughout his childhood. Then, when he became a star, it turned into his trademark. In 1921, Paramount Pictures paid Arbuckle an unheard of three million dollars over three years to produce eighteen movies, then...

He hosted a party at the posh St. Francis Hotel in San Francisco in early September 1921. There was a lot of drinking, and one of the guests, a beautiful young starlet named Virginia Rappe, died several days later from an affliction that started at the party.

An autopsy showed the girl died of peritonitis, and it was assumed the death was brought on by drinking and a possible fall. However, Bambina Maude Delmont, Virginia Rappe's friend and a guest at the party, pointed the finger of suspicion at Arbuckle. She swore out a complaint charging him with the girl's death.

Arbuckle was tried three times. The first jury came in deadlocked, so the judge declared a mistrial. The second trial commenced on January 11, 1922. Once again, the jury was deadlocked, and the judge declared a mistrial. Arbuckle's third trial began on March 13, 1922. Finally, on April 12, the jury deliberated less than ten minutes before returning a verdict of not guilty.

They felt terrible for the debacle and apologized to Arbuckle, saying "a great injustice has been done to him." Moreover, "the happening at the hotel was an unfortunate affair for which Arbuckle, so the evidence shows, was in no way responsible."

Here's how it all came about.

Roscoe Arbuckle drove into San Francisco with friends Lowell Sherman and Fred Fishback in his $34,000 (nearly $500,00 today) Pierce-Arrow Model 66 touring car. The boys were looking to blow off a little steam over the Labor Day weekend, so they rented three rooms at the St. Francis Hotel. Arbuckle and Fishback shared room 1219, Sherman took room 1221, and room 1220 was reserved as a party room.

Arbuckle opted for comfortable clothes and wore his pajamas, robe, and slippers when the guests arrived and stayed like that throughout the party. Another guest, Bambina Maude Delmont, decided to join the fun and donned a pair of men's pajamas, which didn't come as a big surprise to anyone. She reportedly drank twelve to fifteen glasses of whiskey in three or four hours.

Roscoe "Fatty" Arbuckle drove into San Francisco with friends Lowell Sherman and Fred Fishback in his $34,000 Pierce-Arrow Model 66 touring car. (San Francisco Examiner. September 11, 1921)

From what guests said, the party was nothing less than a booze-driven orgy. Lowell Sherman, a cinema villain, told detectives, "the refreshments consisted of a very fine quality of Scotch whiskey and an equally fine quality of gin."[176]

"There were five men and four girls in the room," said Delmont. "All were drinking freely. Then, during the afternoon, the party became rough, and Arbuckle showed the effects of drinking. He came in [their room], pulled Virginia into his room, and locked the door."

Delmont heard fighting and screaming for nearly an hour. Finally, when Arbuckle opened the door, Virginia appeared badly beaten. Virginia Rappe was "disheveled and semi-conscious."

Alice Blake, a showgirl, arrived at the party at about 3 p.m. She said Arbuckle and Rappe were seated together on a settee, laughing, and talking. After a while, they ordered food and continued talking.

Alice went to Zey Prevost's room for a few minutes. When she returned, Arbuckle and Virginia had disappeared into room 1219.

"About a half hour later, Mrs. Delmont tried to get into the room, but the door was locked. She banged and banged on the door, and Arbuckle came out. As he opened the door, we heard Miss Rappe moaning and crying, 'I am dying! I am dying!'

"Arbuckle came out, sat down with us, and said: 'Go in and get her dressed and take her back to the Palace [hotel]. She makes too much noise.'"

Alice walked into the room with Delmont and Prevost. Virginia Rappe was lying on the bed, naked and crying.

Unsure what to do, they gave her bicarbonate of soda, but that only made her vomit. So, they poured a cold bath and put her in it.

Next, they tried to dress her but couldn't. Virginia's clothes were shredded as if they were torn from her body. So, they took her to another room and called the hotel physician.

The girls made it seem like Arbuckle attacked Virginia Rappe, but Harry Boyle, the assistant manager, told a different, less sinister story. He said Delmont called out, "A woman is hysterical up here and is tearing her clothes off. You had better do something about it."[177]

When Boyle knocked on the door, Arbuckle let him in. Virginia Rappe was lying on the bed, nearly nude and unconscious.

"Their story was that the young woman had three drinks and had become hysterical. There were several bottles in evidence, and I took it for granted that there was nothing more serious than a drinking party," continued Boyle. "Mrs. Delmont wanted another room for Miss Rappe, and she was placed in bed."[178] Arbuckle carried her halfway to the new room. When he tired, Boyle took her the rest of the way and placed her in the bed.

The guests said nothing about an attack when they talked to Boyle. Dr. M. E. Rumwell, the attending physician, said Virginia's body showed no signs of violence. However, she had minor bruises on her arm and knee, probably caused by a fall. He couldn't say for sure, but he didn't see anything that indicated foul play.

"It was undoubtedly a case of peritonitis," said Rumwell. "A post-mortem showed it was caused by a rupture of the wall at the top of the bladder."

No one said anything about a criminal attack immediately after the incident. The police weren't involved, and no one kept Arbuckle from leaving town. He checked out the following day and returned to Los Angeles. When he learned that Virginia Rappe had died, Arbuckle called the police and agreed to take the next train to San Francisco.

Virginia Rappe, a 25-year-old starlet, died four days after attending a party at the St. Francis Hotel thrown by "Fatty" Arbuckle. Peritonitis was listed as the official cause of death, but detectives suspected Arbuckle hurt Rappe while trying to rape her. (Los Angeles Examiner. September 11, 1921.)

Later, after Delmont learned that Rappe had died, she told reporters, "The brute! I don't see why such men are permitted to live."[179]

Preliminary Hearing

The preliminary hearing was held from September 22 through September 28. When it ended, Arbuckle was held on a charge of manslaughter. However, he was released the following day after posting $5,000 bail and returned to Los Angeles.

Al Semnacher, Virginia Rappe's manager, testified that he collected the girl's torn garments after she was moved to another room. He intended to use them to clean his automobile and tease her for getting drunk and tearing off her clothes.[180] He didn't know they would be needed for evidence. He left town the day after the party when it looked like Virginia was improving.

Arbuckle made a statement to the police on September 10. "Miss Rappe had taken a few drinks," he said. "She became hysterical and complained she could not breathe, then started to tear off her clothes. I requested two girls present at the time to take care of Miss Rappe. She was disrobed and placed in a bathtub to be revived."

When that didn't help, he phoned the manager and requested a separate room for her. Later, he called for a physician.[181]

At the coroner's inquest, Dr. Rumwell said Delmont never said a word "about screams, scuffles, or anything like that" while he was there.

Dr. Kaarboe examined Virginia Rappe at the St. Francis Hotel. "When I got there," he said, "I saw Arbuckle. "'This woman has had too much party,' he said. "'Too much booze, I guess.'" I examined her body down to the waist," continued Kaarboe, "and saw no marks. She was nude to the waist."[182]

Dr. S. P. Strange found eleven bruises on the body when he performed the autopsy a few days later. That conflicted with Dr. Rumwell, who noted one bruise. However, at the trial, Strange admitted he wasn't sure if the bruises were made when Virginia Rappe was still alive or after her death. So, there was no way to say Arbuckle attacked Virginia Rappe based on the bruises.

Nurse Jean Jameson spoke with Virginia Rappe the day after the party. Virginia had been having internal troubles for the past six weeks and wondered if something inside her was broken.

"I'm going to make Arbuckle pay for this," Virginia told her, "because it is his fault."[183] However, she didn't elaborate on what Arbuckle did or why it was his fault.

Another nurse, Vera Cumberland, said Virginia told her she had improper relations with Arbuckle but did not say if they were voluntary or involuntary.

Lowell Sherman, a cinema villain, told detectives, "the refreshments consisted of a very fine quality of Scotch whiskey and an equally fine quality of gin." (San Francisco Examiner. September 13, 1921.)

Al Semnacher visited Virginia the day after the party. He wasn't sure what happened, but Virginia told him, "Roscoe hurt me."

Bambina Maude Delmont never testified at the preliminary hearing or any of the trials. However, her statement that was read at the preliminary hearing seemed to contradict what she told the police when she swore out a warrant against Arbuckle. "We all rushed in and saw Virginia lying on the bed, tearing at her clothes," said Delmont. She was "moaning that she was dying."[184]

Virginia was fully dressed when Zey Prevost and Delmont entered the room. "She was lying on the bed screaming. She declared she was dying," and then "she tore her own clothes off in a frenzy of pain."

The girls said that when Virginia continued screaming after they gave her a cold bath, Arbuckle told her to "stop, or he would throw her out of the window."[185]

Irene Morgan, a former nurse in World War I, had worked as a housekeeper for Harry Lehrman, Virginia Rappe's fiancée, for seven months while Virginia lived with him. She said Virginia often screamed and carried on as she did at the hotel and often tore her clothes off. Sometimes, she would run out of the house half-naked. The spells usually followed a drinking bout, such as at the St. Francis Hotel.[186]

When she finished testifying, Morgan said Frank O'Connell, an investigator for the district attorney's office, had tried to discourage her from being a defense witness. He told her it could damage her character. O'Connell later denied the charge.

First Trial

Arbuckle's first trial opened on November 14, 1921. It went to the jury on December 2.

Most of the testimony paralleled what was given at the coroner's inquest and preliminary hearing. For example, Minnie Neighbours testified that she saw Virginia Rappe at the Wheeler Hot Springs in August. She was acting hysterically and tearing her clothes off.[187]

Dr. Olaf Kaarboe, the first physician to examine Virginia Rappe, said he asked Delmont if the patient had suffered an injury. She told him that "it was simply a case of too much liquor."

Arbuckle spent over two hours on the witness stand during the last days of the trial. He saw chunks of ice on the bed. So, he picked one up and asked Delmont, "What's the idea?"

Delmont told him to put it back. She was running the show. And then, "she tried to order me to leave the room," said Arbuckle.

"If you don't shut up," he retorted, "I'll throw you out of the window."[188]

That helped explain two rumors blown out of proportion in the papers. One said that Arbuckle simulated the sex act with Virginia Rappe using ice cubes. Instead, Bambina Maude Delmont rubbed ice cubes on Virginia Rappe's stomach and chest, trying to comfort her. A few papers took the rumor a step further, saying Arbuckle raped Virginia Rappe with a pop or whiskey bottle.

The papers also portrayed Arbuckle as a heartless monster, threatening to throw Virginia Rappe out the window if she didn't shut up. However, the truth was he told Delmont he'd throw her out the window. The words had nothing to do with Virginia Rappe.

Defense attorney Gavin McNabb cited several instances of witness tampering in his summation. For example, Alice Blake was threatened with jail time unless she signed a declaration saying she heard Virginia Rappe screaming, "I am dying! I am dying! He killed me."

Finally, she signed a statement saying that she heard Virginia say, "I am dying. He hurt me."[189] That was the most she was willing to say, and it was under duress.

Zey Prevost had been subjected to the same threats.[190]

McNabb ended his case by saying, "The purpose of the District Attorney is to discover evidence—not to create it."[191]

In the end, the jury was deadlocked. So, the judge ordered a new trial.

Second Trial

Several key witnesses recanted their testimony at Arbuckle's second trial. Zey Prevost said Virginia Rappe never used the words "he hurt me," at least as they referred to Arbuckle. After Fred Fishback carried Virginia from the cold bath, she had "said something about someone hurting her." She assumed Virginia was talking about Fishback manhandling her when he got her out of the tub. She didn't say anything about Arbuckle hurting her.

"I'm telling the truth now," she said. The district attorney had kept Alice Blake and her locked away against their will for nearly two and a half months before the first trial.

Alice Blake admitted that she did not see Arbuckle or Virginia Rappe enter his bedroom. She just saw them walking toward the door. (San Francisco Examiner. January 14, 1922.)

Alice Blake also admitted that she did not see Arbuckle or Virginia Rappe enter his room. She just saw them walking toward the door. Then, she went to Zey Prevost's room. They came back less than fifteen minutes later. That's when she heard Maude Delmont knocking on the door and asking Arbuckle to open it.

That was a far cry from the hour Maude Delmont said they were locked in there.

District Attorney Mathew Brady shook his head after Alice Blake and Zey Prevost changed their testimony. "The whole trouble with this case," he said, "is that the defendant is rich and influential and has powerful friends and backing."[192]

Several more witnesses testified about Virginia Rappe's strange attacks after having a few drinks. Eugene Presbrey, an author, said the actress went into hysterics after downing two drinks. He finally calmed her down by administering chopped ice.

"I was a fool to drink," said the actress afterward. "It always affects me that way."

J. M. Covington, the owner of the Ship Cafe at Venice, recalled Virginia Rappe shrieking and tearing off her clothes after a few drinks. Frances Bates employed Virginia Rappe as a model at a fashion show in Santa Ana. "The girl writhed and moaned, shrieked and tore several expensive gowns."[193]

And then there was Maude Delmont. She was another problem for the prosecution. Delmont swore out the complaint that allowed the district attorney to charge Arbuckle with manslaughter, but he never put her on the stand.

District Attorney Matthew Brady explained that "the reason he didn't call Maude Delmont to the stand was simple. The investigation of Miss Delmont, her activities in the case, and analysis of her story convinced us that in some particulars, at least she was not telling the truth. In other words, she was an unreliable witness, and we were unwilling that anyone, whether it was Mr. Arbuckle or any other man or woman charged with a crime, should be convicted upon any testimony coming from a witness in who we had no confidence."[194]

Or, put more simply, Bambina Maude Delmont would prove an embarrassment on the witness stand. She had worked as a madam and con woman and had been known to dabble in blackmail. And then, as the first trial ended on December 10, she was charged with bigamy.[195]

After listening to over a month of testimony, the jury could not decide on a verdict, so the judge dismissed them and set a new trial date.

The *San Francisco Examiner* interviewed the six jury members who felt Arbuckle was guilty. They all believed the stories told by Alice Blake and Zey Prevost. Their presentations were honest and straightforward. On the other hand, none of them believed Arbuckle. "The fact that Arbuckle did not take the stand impressed me with the belief that he was afraid to do so," said juror Nathaniel Friedman.

Juror Matthew McGowan was "astonished at the weakness of the case presented by the defense." He felt the "facts presented by the prosecution left no doubt" about Arbuckle's responsibility for her death.[196]

Roscoe Conkling Arbuckle came "dangerously near conviction" in his second trial. Only two jurors stood between him and a guilty verdict; now, a third trial was pending.

Third trial

The *San Francisco Examiner* said the jury returned a not-guilty verdict in less than three minutes. They determined there was "not a scintilla of evidence to show that Arbuckle in any way had been responsible for the injuries that caused the death of the motion picture actress."

"Acquittal is not enough for Roscoe Arbuckle," said the jurors.

"We feel that a great injustice has been done him. We feel also that it was only our plain duty to give him this exoneration, under the evidence, for there was not the slightest proof adduced to connect him in any way with the commission of a crime.

"He was mainly throughout the case and told a straightforward story on the witness stand, which we all believed.

"The happening at the hotel was an unfortunate affair for which Arbuckle, so the evidence shows, was in no way responsible.

"We wish him success and hope that the American people will take the judgment of fourteen men and women who have sat listening for twenty-one days to the evidence that Roscoe Arbuckle is entirely innocent and free from all blame."[197]

Two weeks after a jury acquitted Arbuckle, Will H. Hays, president of the Motion Picture Producers and Distributors, Inc., pulled all Fatty Arbuckle's films from the American screen. In effect, he punished Arbuckle and the studios for something beyond their control.

Hay's decision would cost Arbuckle and the studios millions in lost revenue. On top of that, the cost of the trials was staggering. The city and county of San Francisco spent $35,000 prosecuting the case. Arbuckle spent over $150,000 on his defense.[198]

The accusations ruined Fatty Arbuckle's career. He was forced to sell his home and Pierce-Arrow touring car to cover his attorney's bills, and he was never able to resurrect his career.

Appendix 1: The Mysterious Murders of San Francisco

*(This article was originally published in the **San Francisco Call** on February 23, 1902. It's a fascinating, albeit hard-to-read, account of old-time murders in San Francisco and how the police approached them. Keep in mind, it's just an outline, but it talks about a dozen murders that baffled Chief Lees over his fifty-year career.)*

"Mysterious murders? Mysterious is a big word," said Chief Lees when I asked him to relate some of the mysterious crimes that had come under his investigation during almost half a century of his term in office.

"Some of the crimes that seem most mysterious are the simplest when unraveled. Lack of complication makes it hard to get at a loose end.

"Then way back of a murder is that mystery of motive.

"Well, tell you one thing, I'm going to do before I pass in my checks and step down and out," said the captain. "I intend to clear up a few mysteries on which I have collected sufficient evidence.

Chief Isaac Lees. (San Francisco Call. November 27, 1910.)

"Of mysterious murders, there may seem on the face of it to be many, but there are few clueless murderers.

"In nearly every case, the murderer stands morally convicted, but there is a distinction between moral conviction and criminal conviction. A man may stand

160

morally convicted before the court and the world, and yet there may not be legal evidence enough to convict him.

"The state fairly wreaks in bloody stench. Now there is the lynching case at Alturas, the case of policeman Robinson's murder in this city, and the case of the four conspirator strikers who killed Rice. The investigation of the Nora Fuller murder adds another chapter to the book of crime.

The cases that I expect to go east to investigate are the hitherto unexplained mysteries to the public of the reign of terror of the tenderloin. I have evidence that I hope to work up to place blame where it belongs."

The murders to which Lees referred were those which terrorized the Whitechapel of San Francisco in February and March 1896. Little May Smith, or Maggie McDermott, as she was known in her district, was found strangled on the early morning of February 10. May Smith was a girl of beauty and young in crime. She was only 20. She had rooms back of a saloon. There were two entrances to her rooms, one through the saloon and one from the side street. As her apartment was anything but exclusive, it was nobody's business, in particular, to notice who entered or left.

The secrecy and, at the same time, the abandon of those of her profession offer scope for undetected midnight murders. History abounds in just such instances. The deed was done, and the murderer escaped. It was not until the collector called for Maggie McDermott's rent that the crime was discovered.

Finger marks on her throat showed how her end had come. The police closely patrolled the streets and cross-questioned everyone they could think of when suddenly, right under their supervision, another, more awful murder shocked the community.

On the morning of March 10, a Frenchman, Caesar Chebart, found Bertha Paradis dead in her rooms. She had been choked to death by means of a large handkerchief which had been forced down her throat with the aid of a carpenter's pencil. Although Caesar Chebart had been living with her, he was obviously the last man to have committed the crime. And as in the Maggie McDermott case, no one had taken cognizance of her visitors.

Chief Lees declares that the curtain has not fallen on the last of this tragedy. "The same person who committed the crimes in San Francisco strangled three women of the same social status in Denver and one in New York."

These statements are pertinent coming as they do in the aftermath of the awful murders whose investigation holds the public attention.

We are restless people—a shifting city of wanderers in this western outpost, through which the tide flows both ways representing every tribe and condition of man. A cosmopolitan city is, by necessity, an unsociable city. No man knows his neighbor. And in such a community, there is always an undercurrent of degradation which gives vent to itself periodically in horrible crimes. The community is shocked, and then those who having eyes see not rub their sightless orbs and stare and gasp, "Can such a thing be!"

"The murderer of Nora Fuller was a moral pervert," declares Captain Lees. "Another Theodore Durrant, who lured his innocent victim on with feasible promises to a place where she would be helplessly in his power, and there he killed her out of lustful wantonness. The scheme had all the deep planning of a Durrant.

"The Durrant case stands out in the annals of crime as being the most atrocious on record. But the chain of circumstantial evidence in the case was absolutely perfect—when they got through with it, not a link missing. Yet, at first, it was enveloped in mystery—as far as the papers and public were concerned. But way back from the public view, the detectives are oftentimes working out clues.

"I hope that in the present case, by dint of closely following each and every clue, the perpetrator of the horrible crime may be discovered.

"That is what ought to be done. No clue is too trivial, no hint too insignificant to follow, for it may open up a field for other theories. Then, when the detectives have built up their theory and are confident it is the right one, something comes in to overthrow it all, and you must start again from the beginning.

"But there are no clueless murders."

A parallel case of a body found in a vacant house occurred in the early 80s. Wright Le Roy pretended he wanted to buy the property of capitalist Skerret and lured him into a vacant house on Ellis Street with the avowed purpose of looking at the house.

A Mr. Dollar, an accomplice, got the key from a neighbor and, to throw off suspicion from Le Roy, engaged the house himself.

The neighbors heard the tacking down of carpets and were convinced that someone had slept in the house. Suspicion was aroused when Le Roy went down to the bank and tried to draw Skerret's money. Investigation brought the horrible fact to light that

Skerret had been strangled in one of the closets of the Ellis Street house.

Those who have visited Chinatown have probably noticed the old house on the northwest corner of California and Dupont Street. It stands back and has a high garden fence which is used as a neighbor sign board for Chinatown guides.

In 1880, Miss Frederica Drell, an old woman, was strangled. She was spoken of for years afterward as "poor old Frederica Drell."

No one was found around the premises, but an old black cat lay curled up sound asleep on the breast of her mistress. Inquiry could bring nothing to light.

The cat must have been the only witness to the deed.

Mystery has always surrounded this deed, "but," said Lees, "Frederica Drell was killed by Lucky Bays, who murdered her for her money."

The murder around which the most impenetrable mystery hangs is that of Eugene Ware, a drug clerk of the Saint Nicholas pharmacy, who was found at 1:15 a.m., December 14, 1894, by police officer O'Day.

O'Day, while patrolling the neighborhood, looked across. He noticed there was no light in the drugstore, which was an unusual circumstance, for even when the store was closed, the light was always burning.

He crossed the street, tried the door, found it unlocked, and walked in. The cash register was open, and various drugs were heaped in confusion.

At the end of the stone steps leading to the basement of the store lay the lifeless body of Ware. Nineteen wounds, evidently made with a sharp, two-edged dagger, lacerated his body. It looked like the work of a maniac.

Then the theory of robbery was advanced, but on investigation, nothing was found to be missing except some small change which might have been spent by Ware himself before he closed up. Clots of blood found at the head of the stairs gave rise to the theory that the murder was committed upstairs and that the body was taken down the steps.

Ware had many female admirers who used to hover about the store and chat with him in the evenings. Among the customers who had noticed this was Miss F. Jackson, who came to the store on the fatal evening to get a headache powder. She testified that a dark-eyed Jewess dressed in black was engaged in conversation with Ware and told him she would "shake" her friend—a man who was waiting for her outside.

Miss Jackson saw her join her friend outside, who seemed to be very angry. Upon these circumstances and the default of a better theory, it was thought that the man, angered by jealousy, returned to the store later and killed the clerk.

Another theory tried to connect Durrant with the murder when his horrible crimes came to light a few months later. It was asserted that Ware and Durrant were friends and were interested in the same girls, but it was denied as many times as it was asserted.

Back in 1876, Jenny Bonnet, the French frog catcher, an eccentric young Frenchwoman who used to bring frogs to the restaurants, was shot and killed at the Eight-Mile House down on the county road.

On the night of the murder, she was rooming with Blanch Buneau, another French woman, and it was thought that the shot was aimed at Blanch. A man named Gerard was arrested but soon released.

"But the real murderer of Jenny Bonnet escaped to Canada," declares Captain Lees, "murdered a man there. Then, just as we had secured evidence and were making arrangements to bring him back, he killed himself, but we got the whole confession out of his wife."

Henry Plans, a young man of 25, who had just been appointed manager of the Fredericksburg Brewery in San

Jose in November 1892, was found hanging from a pepper tree on Julian Street near the bridge.

The body was discovered by John F. Sullivan, a night watchman, at the broad-gauge depot. He was going home at 6:15 on the morning of the 12th and, on crossing a vacant lot, looked up and saw this ghastly tragedy hanging in front of him.

Evidence on the road and shoes showed the body had been carried for some distance before it was hanged.

The first theory was the anarchist suggestion: There was the midnight assassination and holding up of the tragedy with a spectacular and semi-boastful effect to a shocked community.

The anarchists at that time in San Jose were banded together against those who did not belong. This theory was further substantiated by the fact that Plans, on his appointment, discharged several men who were supposed to be anarchists, and November 11, the night of the murder, is the anniversary of the Haymarket riots and a day sacred to the cause of anarchy.

And on such flimsy threads as these are theories built up and torn down in the face of evidence from a different source and of a different nature.

"Lost his life in the discharge of duty" is the statement that halos six of our police officers. John Runk paid for his crime in the extreme penalty of the law. He shot Charles J. Coots, a substitute officer, in April 1877 and was hanged for the same crime one year later.

Officer Nicholson was stabbed in the neck by an unknown Chinese burglar near the corner of Mason and Pacific Streets in February 1884. The Chinaman got in the grocery store over a transom. When he came out, he had a clock and started to run. Nicholson ran after him. A witness who had not yet reached the corner could not testify that he saw the murder, but he heard the shots from the police officer's revolver. The Chinaman had a chisel with which he stabbed Nicholson in the jugular vein. The clock was found in an empty lot. The Chinaman was caught, but the evidence was lacking. The only witness merely heard the shots and did not see the murder.

Under the head of mysterious murders in the records comes that of Edward J. Osgood, who was found with a knife wound in the neck inflicted by an unknown assassin. His body was found at 3:30 a.m., December 13, 1886, at the corner of Pacific and Dupont Streets, so says the record. But ex-Chief Lees says he was stabbed by an English sailor, who, after the crime, boarded a ship and went to Portsmouth, England. Unfortunately, the city at that time did not have the contingent funds to make the trip and investigate the affair legally, and the mayor ordered the matter dropped.

And so, things go down to posterity as mysteries!

Lieutenant William Lee Burke was shot on Bernal Heights in March 1896, and Haynes, his murderer, was sentenced to life imprisonment.

Another mystery case that is still pending is that of officer Eugene Robinson who died from a gunshot wound received while trying to arrest a trio of footpads at the corner of Valencia and Sixteenth Streets.

"In the case of the murder of Alexander Grant, an officer of police, M. B. Curtis, was the murderer, and you can say that I said so. I think that every fair-minded man thinks so, too," said Lees emphatically. "He stands morally convicted before the world, and wherever he may go is morally branded as a murderer. M. B. Curtis, alias Maurice B. Strellinger, killed Alexander Grant, but he was acquitted.

"Why was he acquitted? I will tell you because he spent $80,000 on the jury."

On the first jury, Hurley disagreed with the others on the murder decision. Then, when the case was appealed,

Curtis bought the jury through his spokesman Hurley; one of the jury up and died.

Miss Nelly Harrington, a spinster about 45 years of age, was murdered in her room on June 1, 1895. The murderer tried to cover up his traces by heaping clothes on the body, saturating them with oil, and setting it all on fire.

The only person who could have furnished any clue to the crime was killed before he had time to make a statement to the police.

Just before the crime, a man was seen to drive up and enter the house of which Nelly Harrington was the landlady. Then, after a time, he was seen to come out and drive away.

Ex-state Senator L. W. Buck was a frequent visitor of hers, and he was summoned from his home in Oakland to tell what he knew. Accompanied by a special officer, he started for the depot in a dog cart, but on the way, the horse shied and threw Buck on the pavement on his head. He was unconscious, and three days later, he died without regaining consciousness or without being able to utter a syllable.

The murder of young Robert C. Hislop in May 1901 was one of the most fiendish pieces of butchery ever known, especially when the youth and helplessness of the victim are taken into consideration.

The murderer stole upon this 13-year-old boy and killed him as he lay in bed. From the position of the body, it was evident that the lad had not even seen his slayer.

No trace of the murderer has ever been found. Only the hatchet which struck the fatal blows was picked up in a vacant lot opposite [the Hislop home].

It was the habit of Mrs. Hislop to walk to her husband's furniture store each evening and accompany him home. Robert usually went with her, but on this particular evening, he said he was tired and went to bed.

When they returned, this horrible crime awaited them.

Mrs. Sadie Carpenter was strangled in a room at the Hubbard House, 139 Fourth Street, in July 1898. Lizzie Riley, who occupied the next room to Miss Carpenter's, heard a noise as if someone was groaning. She notified the night clerk, but when the room was entered, Sadie Carpenter was dead. The woman was found in bed, a piece of calico tied tightly around her throat.

No theories held together strong enough to give evidence to point out the murderer.

George Howard, an expressman, was found stabbed near Chinatown in 1879. The murder was not cleared up, but evidence showed that it was the work of a highbinder.

About this time, the body of the little two-year-old son of Antonio Pocceridio, an Italian gardener, was found in a potato patch with the throat cut from ear to ear.

Father Kedrovianski was found about this time in a doorway. He was in a stupefied condition and died soon afterward. The crime could not be fixed on anyone.

Little Pete was shot by highbinders in Chinatown, but no one was singled out or punished. The See Yup Society of Chinatown was at variance with the Sam Yup, and one of the best-known characters of Chinatown was shot. Little Pete was wealthy, looked up to, and feared by the whole of Chinatown and many of the white politicians and bosses.

Dr. J. Milton Bowers was convicted and sentenced to death for the murder of his wife. He was a man of many wives. Cecilia, his fourth wife, died under circumstances that pointed toward poisoning. Investigation proved that his three other wives died suddenly and that in each case, he won the new wife before her predecessor was dead. Cecelia Bowers was insured for about $14,000 in favor of her husband.

Bowers was arrested, tried, convicted, and sentenced to death. While in jail, his brother-in-law Henry Benhayon was found dead in a Gary Street lodging house. It was supposed to be suicide, but in letters he left, he accused his dead sister of unfaithfulness to her husband and confessed that he had committed her murder.

It developed that Benhanyon had not committed suicide but was the pivot of a plot to free Dr. Bowers. Moreover, John Dimmig was suspected of being an accomplice of Bowers. He had rented the room where Benhanyon died, and in the trial, it developed that Dimmig had spent much time writing with the dead man over whom he exercised a strong influence.

The Bowers case involved one to five murders, unexplained as far as the law is concerned, and unsatisfied in punishment. Bowers was finally released, and Dimmig was acquitted.

Appendix 2: Tales of the Highbinders

*(This article about the Highbinders, or criminal idlers, of San Francisco was originally published in the **Los Angeles Herald** on October 14, 1906.)*

Among the problems of rebuilding sanitation, rearrangement of streets, and police regulations now before the authorities of San Francisco, not the least important in the judgment of the local police is the disposition of the criminal element in the city's enormous Chinese population. Tales of crime, actual occurrences, besides which the "Queen of Chinatown" and other melodramatic performances, inane and feeble, were matters of almost daily talk among the San Francisco police before the earthquake and fire destroyed the densely crowded district known as Chinatown. One who has made a study of the conditions that existed in this district says:

Out of the 25,000 Chinese in San Francisco prior to the earthquake and fire, fully 3,000 were believed by the police and the immigration inspectors to be highbinders or criminal idlers. These criminals confined their operations to their own race, levying blackmail at will and punishing with death those who refused to pay. They were thoroughly organized into fifteen tongs or societies, which were known respectively as Kung Tong, Suey On Tong, Bow On Tong, Hop Sing Tong, Hip Sing Tong, Bing Gung Tong, Bow Sin Sere Tong, Gi Sui Sere Tong, Hip Ye Tong, Quong Duck Tong, Jo Lung Sen Tong, Lin On Tong and Jew Ye Tong. None of these tongs were connected in any way with the "Six Companies" or other Chinese commercial organizations.

A Corps of Hatchet Men

Each tong had its corps of hatchet men sworn to murder all who incurred the displeasure of the societies. And so great was the terror they inspired that law-abiding Chinamen could not be depended upon to resist their demand or report their offenses. A system of electric bells, from house to house, and block to block, warned the hatchet men of the approach of a policeman, and sometimes they did not hesitate to shoot down their victim on the street and in daylight, with a policeman nearby so confident were they that the neighbors' fear would insure them from detection.

The tongs were freely charged by the authorities with trying their victims in secret, and in the absence of the latter, and sometimes, with committing murder for pay. They were also said to review and nullify the judgments of the local courts with regard to their proposed victims and, at times, use the local courts to enforce their own decisions. There is on record a trial of a Chinaman for murder in which it was learned, after the conviction of the accused, that all the evidence was false and was furnished by the tongs, which had marked an innocent man for destruction. Even innocent and well-meaning Chinamen were terrified into swearing away the life of fellow countrymen.

Girls at Auction

Among other crimes charged to the tongs was the importation of Chinese girls for questionable purposes and their sale at auction right in the city of San Francisco. As much as three thousand dollars in gold is said to have been realized by a tong for one girl. The maintenance of many gambling rooms, and fully three-fourths of all the violations of the Chinese exclusion law, were also charged to these organizations.

Many of the hatchet men or assassins were ostensibly merchants, but the disguise, in many cases, was transparent. J. D. Putman, an inspector of Chinese immigrants, is an authority for the statement. "There is not one out of ten Chinese in San Francisco styling themselves as merchants and so registered who are merchants, except in name. There are many firms claiming to have from $10,000-$15,000 capital and having a list filed in the custom house of from five to fifteen partners whose stock could be removed at one time in a single express wagon. Usually, there are one or two men found about the store, the rest cooking or gardening or running gambling rooms until just before they wish to visit China, and still, they have no trouble in procuring signers to their papers as being bona fide merchants.

Police Lieutenant William Price declared that after twenty-one years of observation as a member of the city police force, he was convinced that all the tongs were organized and maintained for the purpose of murder and that inoffensive Chinese merchants were obliged to assist in maintaining the tongs to secure immunity from the hired assassins and blackmailers. He also said that these criminal societies have their meeting rooms finely fitted up, and any member at any of the secret meetings may offer a sum of money for the murder of any Chinaman he dislikes.

The hatchet men are immediately blindfolded. Then they draw lots for the selection of the one to commit the desired murder. Two are generally chosen, and they are bound to kill their man, even if a score of policemen be about when they meet him.

Before they go on their errand of murder, the hatchet men fix up what little business they have, just as a white man makes his will before going on a long journey. If the murderer is caught, he is defended at the expense of the tong. If he is imprisoned or hanged, the tong compensates his relatives in China.

Blackmail is levied on the slightest provocation, Lieutenant Price said. He told this story as an illustration. "One evening, a Chinese butcher in San Francisco threw a little clean water into the street, and a Chinese highbinder standing nearby got a little water in his sleeve.

"When I passed by, the highbinder went into the butcher's store and demanded one hundred dollars as atonement for the offense. I learned of the demand and told the butcher not to pay the money but to arrange to meet the highbinder at a certain place, and I would be there. He promised to do so, and I left him, but before I returned to his store, he had paid the hundred dollars out of sheer fear of his life."

Descent on the Tongs

At one time, backed by the chief of police and encouraged by the Chinese Consul, Lieutenant Price took sixteen men in uniform with axes. They destroyed the rooms of five of the tongs. They literally cut the furniture to pieces making kindling wood of about $180,000 worth of property.

Wherever the squad went, it found arms, ammunition, Bowie knives two feet long in blade, iron bars done up in braided cord, and chain and steel armor, the latter to be worn under the clothing. One joss, or idol, they destroyed had been brought from China and was worth seven or eight hundred dollars. In another building, there were seven josses, and all these were destroyed, greatly to the consternation of the friendly Chinamen, who predicted the lieutenant's death. The lieutenant still lives to tell the story of the raids. As a result of this vigorous action, several of the tongs were driven out of San Francisco, and for three years, there was not a Chinaman killed in the city.

The hatchet man, according to the lieutenant, seldom carries a pistol but is accompanied by another that Chinamen call "jury," who carries the weapon and passes it to the hatchet man at the opportune time for the crime. When the fatal shot is fired, the pistol is quickly passed to the "jury," who disappears. The highbinder, if caught, quietly submits to having his pockets searched by the police.

While the lieutenant and two policemen were on one side of the street, and two policemen were on the other side, a hatchet man walked up to his victim, an old Chinese merchant, and repeatedly plunged a knife ten inches long into the old man's body. This murderer was, of course, caught red-handed, but the incident showed that the highbinder was obliged to kill his man without regard to the consequences.

A Murderer's Commission

Dr. J. Endicott Gardner, an interpreter of Chinese who has spent more than thirty years of life among Chinamen at home and in San Francisco, possesses a letter of instructions to a highbinder or salaried soldier. It reads as follows:

To Lum Hip, salaried officer:

It has been said that to plan schemes and devise methods and hold the seal is the work of the literary class, while to oppose foes, fight battles, and plant firm government, is the work of the military.

Now this tong appoints salaried soldiers to be ready to protect ourselves and assist others. This is our object.

All, therefore, who undertake the military service of this tong must obey orders, and without orders, you must not dare to act. If any of our brethren are suddenly molested, it will be necessary for you to act with resolute well.

You should always work in the interest of the tong and never make your office a means of private revenge.

When orders are given, you shall advance valiantly to your assigned task. Never shrink or turn your back on the battlefield.

When a ship arrives in port with women on board, and the grandmaster issues an order for you to go down and receive them, you must be punctual and use all your ability for the good of the commonwealth (or state).

If in the discharge of your duty you are slain, we will undertake to pay five hundred dollars sympathy money to your friends.

If you are wounded, a doctor will be engaged to heal your wounds, and if you are incapacitated for any length of time, you will receive ten dollars a month.

If you are maimed for life and incapacitated for work, two hundred and fifty dollars shall be paid to you, and a subscription taken to defray the costs of your journey home to China.

This paper is given as proof, as word of mouth may not be believed.

Furthermore, whenever you exert your strength to kill or wound enemies of this tong and in so doing, you are arrested or imprisoned, one hundred dollars per year shall be paid to your friends during your imprisonment.

Dated 13th day of 5th month of 14th year. Kwong Sui, Victoria, B. C. (Seal of Chee Kong Tong).

Girl's Terrible Tale

Dr. Gardner also possesses a catechism used in the coaching of witnesses for the landing of Chinese slave girls.

Miss Donaldina Cameron, the matron of the Presbyterian Chinese Rescue Home in San Francisco, estimated that 90% or more of the Chinese girls brought to San Francisco were destined for immoral lives. She said these girls were bought and paid for in China. Then, they were compelled to take the purchase money into their own hands and give it to the person selling them so it could not come back upon the person making the purchase.

One of these girls rescued by the home was blind, having been made so by imprisonment in a chicken coop, where vermin destroyed her sight. This imprisonment was a punishment inflicted upon her by the highbinders for some act of disobedience.

Deportation of every Chinaman found to be a member of a Highbinders' society is believed by authorities to be the only remedy for a criminal condition that is probably without a parallel in any other city in the world.

Research Methodology

Sometimes it's fun to watch a story unfold as it did for contemporary readers.

I like to write my historical works, relying mainly on old newspaper accounts. But newspaper accounts are problematic. Often no two reports are precisely alike. One reporter starts the story. A thousand more jump in and add dialogue or change scenes to fit their needs.

When that happens, you must return to personal accounts, public records, and contemporary and current history books. Local history books are somewhat murkier. A lot of great information is available only in the county history books published between 1876 and 1909. The editors of these books went out and collected information straight from the horse's mouth, so to speak. The authors talked with the old pioneers before they passed on.

That was good and bad.

The story is only as good as the person's memory. As a result, dates get mixed up, quotes may not be a hundred percent accurate, and names become a total jumble of misspelled words. That goes double for old newspaper accounts. Frontier editors didn't have spell-check. They sounded words out, and if their hearing was off, the spelling became more convoluted and impossible to follow from article to article.

That makes it doubly hard on modern-day researchers. Newspaper databases require exact matches. If the spelling is off—even by one letter—you will miss the best parts of the story because they're not going to pop up in search.

It's sad but true.

You can get around the misspellings, the wrong dates, and other inaccuracies, but it takes a lot of work. First, you must search for every term, right, and wrong. That means you need to type in every possible misspelling. Next, you need to put yourself in a frontier editor's place and consider what terms he would use to describe things. And, sometimes, you need to go with your gut. Type in a thousand search terms, and you're bound to strike black gold.

Then, when the results pop up, it's tempting to look only at the larger articles, but you miss so much by doing that. Often the smaller pieces have the perfect quote or that missing tidbit of information you are looking for.

You need to go the extra mile.

The information is out there. It all comes down to knowing how to access it.

Chronicling America from the Library of Congress is the most accessible newspaper source. It has thousands of papers online from 1789 to the present day. The good thing is they are all searchable by year, topic, or keywords. When the database pulls up results, it highlights keywords to make locating information easy.

If your time is limited, or you just need to grab a few quick quotes, stick with *Chronicling America*. You will want to go wide if you need a paper not included in the Library of Congress collection.

Recently I've become a big fan of **newspapers.com**. It's a little pricey, but they have many newspapers missing from the Chronicling History site. If you're looking for small-town papers, it's a must-have. Newspaperarchvies.com is another must-visit site. It contains many papers not available on Chronicling History or newspapers.com.

Google News is another great site that offers complete copies of vintage newspapers. From my perspective, Google News is not as user-friendly as

Chronicling America or **newspapers.com**, but they provide many papers the Library of Congress does not have.

Google News makes it easy to check a complete run of one newspaper or to blast through a week's or a month's worth of stories as they develop.

So, it pays to check all three sites.

No serious researcher can get by without **Google Books**. It is a one-stop shop for just about every book you could wish for. Ever since I stumbled across Google Books, going to the library has dropped off my to-do list.

If you still can't find the book you want, Google it. Many local history projects have transcribed full books or sections of books and added them to their websites.

It's crazy but true. Just about every reference source you want is available on the internet.

Another source I enjoy is the **Making of America** series from Cornell University. It's my go-to source for old magazines such as *Harper's New Monthly Magazine*, *Scribner's*, the *North American Review,* and more.

If you are researching the civil war, Making of America contains a digitized/searchable version of the *Official Records of the Union and Confederate Armies and Navies*.

Some stories are so good, you want to get them out, but nothing—the trail goes dead. The source material just fades away.

I do not know how many stories I've started and had to stop because the source material dried up.

What I do requires vintage newspapers and court documents, but sometimes they disappear or are destroyed by fire, or they have not been digitized yet, so they are next to impossible to find.

It's disappointing, but it's part of the game. You move on to the next story.

Here's a great story from Clinton, Iowa, that fizzled out as I wrote *Gruesome Quad-Cities*.

John Taylor grew tired of his wife Annie and enlisted the help of two prostitutes, Annie Underhill and Jennie Grey, to help solve his problem.

The simple version of the story is they poisoned her. They would have gotten away with it, too, except two days after killing his wife, John married Annie Underhill.

That got his neighbors thinking—maybe John killed his wife so he could marry his prostitute friend.

At first, the doctors were on his side. They said Annie died from heart disease. And that's the way it would have gone down in history, except a neighbor woman told authorities she heard Annie screaming and ran to her side. Mrs. Taylor said, "she'd been poisoned."

The woman got the information to the doctor before the woman's burial, but he ignored it. Instead, he insisted Annie's death was due to an enlarged heart, and it would have stayed that way except for the neighbor's persistence.

She searched the house and found some suspicious powder she took to Dr. McCormick for analysis. He determined it was strychnine.[199]

Annie Taylor's body was exhumed the next week, and the heart and liver were removed. Dr. McCormick and several other experts performed a chemical analysis of the organs and discovered enough strychnine in the woman's stomach to kill her.

Based on that information, C. C. Wood of Riverside swore out a warrant for Taylor's arrest.[200]

John Taylor confessed to Sheriff Purcell two days after his arrest. He wanted to get rid of his wife to marry Annie Underhill.

Annie Underhill "assisted him by procuring the poison and mixing up the powder. She handed the fatal doses to him with the remark—they would finish her."[201] Another prostitute named Jennie Grey watched as she mixed the poison. When Annie finished mixing the potion, Grey said, "Yes, they'll do away with her."

Taylor later recanted his confession at the coroner's inquest.

Based on Taylor's testimony, Sheriff Purcell arrested the two women. He locked Annie Taylor up in the Lyon's Jail and secured Jennie Grey in a local tramp house.

On August 13, the coroner's jury found John Taylor and Annie (Underhill) Taylor guilty of poisoning his wife, Annie.

Annie Underhill said she knew nothing about the murder, but her friend Jennie Wheeler said differently. Annie showed her John and Annie's wedding license the week before she died and said she would soon be John's wife.[202]

The jury was out 33 hours in the Annie (Underhill) Taylor case and returned a verdict of guilty of murder in the first degree. She was sentenced to life imprisonment.

After her conviction, John Taylor surprised everyone when he pleaded guilty. Judge Hager charged the jury with determining the degree of the crime because a new Iowa law forced the jury to decide between hanging and imprisonment.[203]

After hearing her sentence, Annie Underhill threw a fit, proclaiming her innocence. John said she was innocent and promised to make a statement later, but the Muscatine Weekly Journal had doubts. "His stories are so conflicting and unreliable," said the paper, "that no dependence can be placed on them."[204]

"This woman here is innocent of anything," whispered Taylor, "is innocent of anything at all about it. She knew nothing."[205]

John got sentenced to life in the Anamosa Prison, and Annie to life in the Fort Madison Prison.

It's such a cool story. You know there is more to it but try finding copies of the *Clinton Herald* for the latter half of 1879.

They do not exist.

The Clinton Public Library's digitized collection is light on the *Clinton Herald*, as is the Library of Congress collection and Newspapers.com.

It hurts to give up, but sometimes you have to do it.

Footnotes

[1] San Francisco Call. April 15, 1895.

[2] San Francisco Call. April 15, 1895.

[3] San Francisco Call. April 15, 1895.

[4] San Francisco Examiner. October 20, 1895.

[5] San Francisco Chronicle. April 18, 1895.

[6] San Francisco Call. May 2, 1895.

[7] San Francisco Call. May 4, 1895.

[8] San Francisco Call. April 18, 1895.

[9] San Francisco Call. April 19, 1895.

[10] San Francisco Call. April 21, 1895.

[11] San Francisco Call. April 20, 1895.

[12] San Francisco Call. April 18, 1895.

[13] San Francisco Call. April 18, 1895.

[14] San Francisco Call. September 19, 1895.

[15] San Francisco Examiner. September 25, 1895.

[16] San Francisco Call. September 4, 1895. The opening day of the trial, including the prosecutor's summation of the case is included in this issue.

[17] San Francisco Call. September 4, 1895.

[18] San Francisco Chronicle. September 12, 1895.

[19] San Francisco Chronicle. September 26, 1895.

[20] San Francisco Call. December 7, 1895.

[21] San Francisco Examiner. January 4, 1898.

[22] This account of Durrant's death is condensed from the San Francisco Examiner. January 8, 1898.

[23] San Francisco Call. January 22, 1899.

[24] San Francisco Call. January 22, 1899.

[25] San Francisco Call. January 22, 1899.

[26] San Francisco Call. January 11, 1899.

[27] San Francisco Call. January 11, 1899.

[28] San Francisco Call. January 11, 1899.

[29] San Francisco Call. April 9, 1900.

[30] San Francisco Call. April 20, 1900.

[31] San Francisco Examiner. July 13, 1900.

[32] San Francisco Call. July 13, 1900.

[33] San Francisco Examiner. April 22, 1900.

[34] San Francisco Examiner. December 17, 1897.
[35] San Francisco Examiner. December 17, 1897.
[36] San Francisco Examiner. December 17, 1897.
[37] Drake, Thomas Samuel. Celebrated Criminal Cases. 1901. P. 126.
[38] San Francisco Examiner. December 19, 1897.
[39] San Francisco Examiner. December 19, 1897.
[40] San Francisco Examiner. December 19, 1897.
[41] San Francisco Examiner. December 19, 1897.
[42] San Francisco Examiner. December 19, 1897.
[43] San Francisco Examiner. December 17, 1897.
[44] San Francisco Examiner. December 23, 1897.
[45] San Francisco Examiner. December 23, 1897.
[46] San Francisco Examiner. December 19, 1897.
[47] San Francisco Examiner. December 24, 1897.
[48] San Francisco Call. December 18, 1897.
[49] San Francisco Examiner. April 3, 1898.
[50] San Francisco Call. August 2, 1899.
[51] San Francisco Call. December 23, 1900.
[52] The Morning News. August 16, 1898.
[53] The Morning News. August 17, 1898.
[54] Daily Republican. July 7, 1898.
[55] The Morning News. September 1, 1898.
[56] San Francisco Call. August 28, 1898.
[57] San Francisco Call. August 30, 1898.
[58] San Francisco Call. August 30, 1898.
[59] San Francisco Call. September 3, 1898.
[60] Some accounts list her name as Almira Ruoff.
[61] San Francisco Chronicle. September 15, 1898.
[62] San Francisco Call. September 4, 1898.
[63] San Francisco Call. September 5, 1898.
[64] San Francisco Call. August 7, 1898.
[65] San Francisco Call. December 20, 1898.
[66] San Francisco Call. December 28, 1898.
[67] San Francisco Call. December 20, 1898.
[68] San Francisco Call. December 20, 1898.
[69] San Francisco Call. December 20, 1898.
[70] San Francisco Examiner. December 29, 1898.
[71] San Francisco Call, December 31, 1898.
[72] San Francisco Call. March 15, 1901.
[73] San Francisco Call. April 8, 1904.
[74] San Francisco Examiner. June 13, 1905.

[75] San Francisco Call. March 8, 1910.

[76] The San Francisco Call. July 18, 1898.

[77] The San Francisco Call. July 26, 1898.

[78] The San Francisco Call. July 26, 1898.

[79] The San Francisco Call. July 23, 1898.

[80] The San Francisco Call. July 18, 1898.

[81] The San Francisco Call. July 23, 1898.

[82] The San Francisco Chronicle. July 27, 1898.

[83] The San Francisco Call. July 27, 1898.

[84] San Francisco Call. May 27, 1901.

[85] San Francisco Examiner. May 30, 1901.

[86] San Francisco Call. May 27, 1901.

[87] San Francisco Call. May 30, 1901.

[88] San Francisco Examiner. June 6, 1901.

[8989] Some early accounts say his name was Harry Schmidt, but as the story progressed reporters settled on Harry Smith.

[90] San Francisco Call. May 27, 1901.

[91] Harry Schmidt in some early accounts.

[92] San Francisco Call. May 29, 1901.

[93] San Francisco Call. May 28, 1901.

[94] San Francisco Call. May 29, 1901.

[95] San Francisco Examiner. June 6, 1901.

[96] San Francisco Call. May 31, 1901.

[97] San Francisco Call. June 4, 1901.

[98] San Francisco Examiner. July 2, 1902.

[99] San Francisco Examiner. January 16, 1902.

[100] San Francisco Examiner. January 19, 1902.

[101] San Francisco Examiner. January 17, 1902.

[102] San Francisco Examiner. February 11, 1902.

[103] San Francisco Examiner. February 11, 1902.

[104] San Francisco Examiner. February 11, 1902.

[105] San Francisco Examiner. February 11, 1902.

[106] San Francisco Examiner. February 11, 1902.

[107] San Francisco Examiner. February 20, 1902.

[108] San Francisco Examiner. February 20, 1902.

[109] San Francisco Examiner. February 20, 1902.

[110] San Francisco Examiner. February 20, 1902.

[111] The San Francisco Call. February 12, 1902.

[112] San Francisco Examiner. February 20, 1902.

[113] San Francisco Examiner. February 20, 1902.

[114] San Francisco Examiner. February 20, 1902.
[115] San Francisco Examiner. February 20, 1902.
[116] The San Francisco Call. March 2, 1902.
[117] The San Francisco Call. March 2, 1902.
[118] San Francisco Examiner. March 15, 1902.
[119] San Francisco Examiner. March 15, 1902.
[120] San Francisco Chronicle. March 15, 1902.
[121] Oakland Tribune. March 5, 1902.
[122] San Francisco Examiner. March 14, 1902.
[123] San Francisco Examiner. March 14, 1902.
[124] Duke, Thomas B. Celebrated Criminal Cases of America. 1910. P. 146.
[125] The San Francisco Call. April 28, 1902.
[126] The San Francisco Call. April 28, 1902.
[127] Duke, Thomas B. Celebrated Criminal Cases of America. 1910. P. 146.
[128] San Francisco Chronicle. July 14, 1902.
[129] The San Francisco Call. January 18, 1904.
[130] The San Francisco Call. January 28, 1904.
[131] The San Francisco Call. January 28, 1904.
[132] The San Francisco Call. January 28, 1904.
[133] The San Francisco Call. January 13, 1904.
[134] The San Francisco Call. January 22, 1904.
[135] The San Francisco Call. January 14, 1904.
[136] The San Francisco Call. January 12, 1904.
[137] The San Francisco Call. January 27, 1904.
[138] The San Francisco Call. January 27, 1904.
[139] The San Francisco Call. January 27, 1904.
[140] The San Francisco Call. February 3, 1904.
[141] The San Francisco Call. February 3, 1904.
[142] The San Francisco Call. February 19, 1904.
[143] The San Francisco Call. May 13, 1904.
[144] The San Francisco Call. May 19, 1904.
[145] The San Francisco Call. May 18, 1904.
[146] The San Francisco Call. September 16, 1904.
[147] The San Francisco Call. October 9, 1906.
[148] The San Francisco Call. January 29, 1907.
[149] The San Francisco Call. March 30, 1907.
[150] San Francisco Examiner. August 1, 1914.
[151] San Francisco Examiner. August 1, 1914.
[152] San Francisco Examiner. August 1, 1914.
[153] San Francisco Examiner. August 1, 1914.
[154] San Francisco Examiner. October 19, 1913.

[155] San Francisco Examiner. January 29, 1914.

[156] San Francisco Chronicle. October 19, 1913.

[157] San Francisco Examiner. October 19, 1913.

[158] San Francisco Examiner. January 31, 1914.

[159] San Francisco Examiner. February 1, 1914.

[160] San Francisco Examiner. August 4, 1911.

[161] San Francisco Examiner. August 4, 1911.

[162] San Francisco Examiner. August 5, 1911.

[163] San Francisco Examiner. August 5, 1911.

[164] San Francisco Chronicle. September 9, 1911.

[165] San Francisco Examiner. December 3, 1911.

[166] San Francisco Examiner. July 24, 1912.

[167] San Francisco Chronicle. February 12, 1913. The paper gave the victim's name as Charles La Salle. No explanation was given for the variance.

[168] San Francisco Chronicle. July 4, 1911.

[169] San Francisco Chronicle. December 6, 1911.

[170] Some accounts say she forgot to load the gun. Others say the gun misfired, so I can the reader can choose which they like better.

[171] San Francisco Examiner. October 26, 1913.

[172] San Francisco Examiner. October 26, 1913.

[173] San Francisco Chronicle. February 25, 1914.

[174] San Francisco Examiner. April 1, 1914.

[175] Stockton Evening & Sunday Record. April 1, 1914.

[176] Los Angeles Evening Post-Record. September 22, 1921.

[177] San Francisco Chronicle. September 10, 1921.

[178] San Francisco Chronicle. September 10, 1921.

[179] San Francisco Chronicle. September 10, 1921.

[180] Chicago Tribune. September 25, 1921.

[181] Chicago Tribune. September 11, 1921.

[182] Chicago Tribune. September 13, 1921.

[183] Chicago Tribune. September 14, 1921.

[184] Chicago Tribune. September 14, 1921.

[185] San Francisco Examiner. September 28, 1921.

[186] San Francisco Examiner. November 26, 1921.

[187] Neighbours was later charged with perjury when the prosecution couldn't find any evidence that proved Virginia Rappe had visited the Wheeler Hot Springs.

[188] San Francisco Examiner. November 29, 1921.

[189] San Francisco Examiner. December 2, 1921.

[190] San Francisco Examiner. December 3, 1921.

[191] San Francisco Examiner. December 3, 1921.

[192] San Francisco Examiner. January 26, 1922.

[193] San Francisco Examiner. January 22, 1922.

[194] San Francisco Chronicle. Jan 21, 1922.

[195] San Francisco Examiner. December 11, 1921.

[196] San Francisco Examiner. February 4, 1922.

[197] San Francisco Examiner. April 13, 1922.

[198] San Francisco Examiner. April 13, 1922.

[199] The Clinton Age. August 8, 1879.

[200] The Clinton Age. August 8, 1879.

[201] The Clinton Age. August 8, 1879.

[202] The Clinton Age. November 21, 1879.

[203] The Daily Democrat. November 24, 1879.

[204] Muscatine Weekly Journal. November 28, 1879.

[205] The Clinton Age. November 28, 1879.

Printed in Great Britain
by Amazon

35151304R00116